P9-BYL-263

THE COSMIC DANCE

An Invitation to Experience Our Oneness

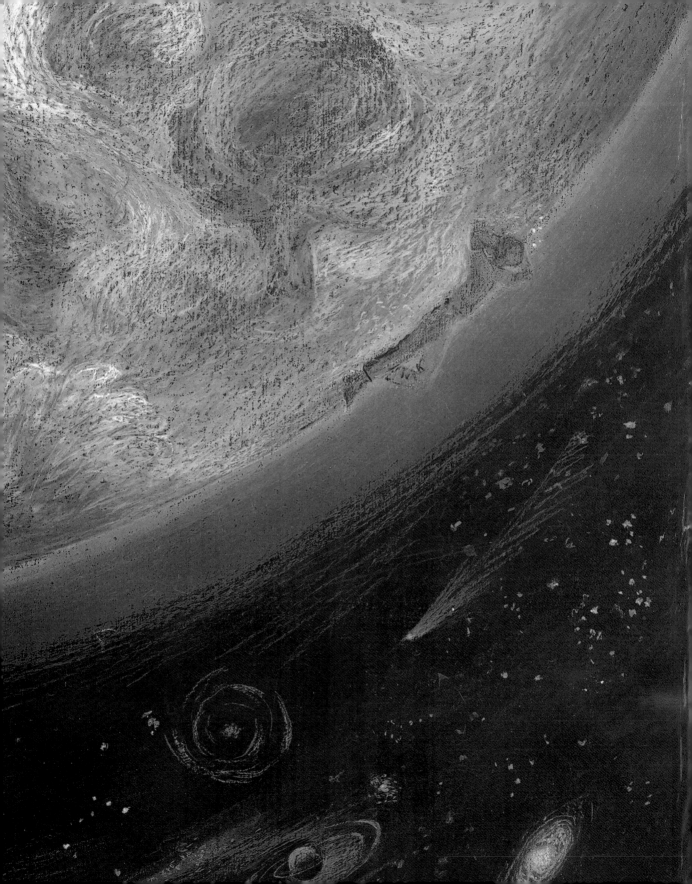

THE COSMIC DANCE
An Invitation to Experience Our Oneness

JOYCE RUPP

ARTWORK BY MARY SOUTHARD

ORBIS BOOKS

Maryknoll, New York 10545

Second printing, April 2003

Founded in 1970, Orbis Books endeavors to publish works that enlighten the mind, nourish the spirit, and challenge the conscience. The publishing arm of the Maryknoll Fathers & Brothers, Orbis seeks to explore the global dimensions of the Christian faith and mission, to invite dialogue with diverse cultures and religious traditions, and to serve the cause of reconciliation and peace. The books published reflect the views of their authors and do not represent the official position of the Maryknoll Society. To learn more about Maryknoll and Orbis Books, please visit our website at www.maryknoll.org.

Text copyright © 2002 by Joyce Rupp

All artwork copyright © 2002 by Mary Southard, CSJ

Published by Orbis Books, Maryknoll, New York, U.S.A.

All rights reserved.

No part of this publication may be reproduced or transmitted in any form or by any means, electronic or mechanical, including photocopying, recording or any information storage or retrieval system, without prior permission in writing from the publisher.

Queries regarding rights and permissions should be addressed to:
Orbis Books, P.O. Box 308, Maryknoll, NY 10545-0308.

Queries on obtaining reproductions of the artwork should be addressed to Mary Southard, Sisters of St. Joseph of La Grange, 1515 West Ogden Avenue, La Grange Park, Illinois 60526-1721.

Manufactured in Italy.

Design: Roberta Savage

Library of Congress Cataloging-in-Publication Data
Rupp, Joyce
      The cosmic dance: an invitation to experience our oneness/Joyce Rupp; artwork by Mary Southard.
         p. cm
      ISBN 1-57075-406-3
         1. Creation—Meditations. 2. Nature—Religious aspects. 3. Spiritual life. I. Title.

BL227 .R87 2002
   242—dc21
                                                                              2001044794

Contents

To Earth,
our life-sustaining planet,
for the wisdom, comfort, and hope
I daily receive
from her generous bounty,
and her astonishing beauty

and

To the Holy One,
Great Dancer of the Cosmos,
whose presence I often sense
as I move among the treasures
of our beloved planet

Acknowledgments

*M*any delightful companions have introduced me to their part of the world and allowed me to taste the beauty and wonder of the cosmos. A number of the experiences I describe in this book come from times when I was a guest of others. Some trekked countless miles with me through varied terrain and territory, stood with me by humming seasides, explored caves and sacred sites, gazed at night skies, sunrises and sunsets, journeyed with me on camping trips, vacations, and retreats. I offer my gratitude especially to Pat Brady, Elizabeth Brennan, Ruth and Frank Butler, Vince Burns, Marge Cashman, Dolores and Jim Curran, Paula D'Arcy, Kateri Duke, Jean Fallon, Sheila Geraghty, Kathy Cosgrove Green, Erin King, Meg Kopish, Keith and Jenny Lightfoot, Aileen Martin, Felicity McKeon, Colm Moorhouse, Kathleen Pruitt, Marie Micheletto, Tom Pfeffer, Mark and Debbie Pfeffer, Chris Ross, Sharon Samek, Margaret Ann and Art Schmidt, Brenda Rose Syzegedy, Liam Tracey, Macrina Wiederkehr, and countless others whose names elude me but whose presence will always remain as a jewel in my experience of the cosmic dance.

I owe immense gratitude to those who've supported me with their prayer, especially Pat Sloan Skinner, Mary Kunkel, Sandra Bury, Janet Barnes, Dorothy Sullivan, Joan and Bernard McLaughlin.

Carola Broderick and Ginny Silvestri lent me their keen eyes and good sense of grammar as they read the initial manuscript. Their suggestions enhanced the text immensely. Catherine Costello and Roberta Savage of Orbis Books gave shape and beauty to the pages. I am blessed to have had their skilled expertise.

What a joy to work with a publisher like Michael Leach. His remarkable enthusiasm and unwavering clarity helped me to keep the theme in focus and to enjoy each part of the manuscript's development.

And Mary Southard! Ever since I first discovered her Earth calendar, the beauty of her art has continually enticed my heart toward greater amazement of our vibrant cosmos. As you gaze upon her art in this book, you will know why I value her vision and art so much.

Thank you, all my readers, who have corresponded with me, supported my work, and have encouraged me to continue to write. I find you all here in *The Cosmic Dance!*

Introduction

The fog has settled in the woods bringing with it a quiet flow of mystery. A red-tailed hawk flies low through the trees, noiseless in her breakfast flight. I stand at the kitchen sink, gazing silently through the window. A tender peace webs its way inside of me as I peer into the milky haze. I feel enfolded in a love much greater than my own. At this moment I lean back in memory and catch a hint of what I knew long ago when I was a small child living on a farm in rural Iowa. It is the melody of the cosmic dance playing in my soul since those early days, a song that has never stopped singing in me.

I never would have named this exquisite bonding quite that way when I was young. But the truth of it was in my bones as I lay on my back looking up at the sparkling sky full of stars and slept overnight on the dew-laden lawn. This hidden dance played in my soul as I fed the chickens each day after school or went down to the barn, climbed the tall ladder to the hay mound, and tossed down hay to the cattle below. This same dance skipped in my spirit when my father, brothers, and I harvested oats and corn. It was there in my mother's presence as I came into the farmhouse on wintry evenings and smelled her delicious chicken soup on the stove. I sensed this dance when I worked with her in the vegetable garden on hot, humid summer days.

As I grew older I lost some of my awareness of the cosmic dance for awhile. I was too focused on a busy life of work and often failed to notice the unspoken mystery in all of creation. But eventually I made some startling discoveries—three of them—and they have changed my life forever. The first of these is the amazing revelation that I am made of stardust, that every part and parcel of who I am materially was once a piece of a star shining in the heavens. The second discovery is that the air I breathe is the air that has circled the globe and been drawn in and out by people, creatures and vegetation in lands and seas far away. But the most astounding discovery that both awakened and affirmed my early childhood awareness is the fact that I am part of a vast and marvelous dance that goes on unceasingly at every moment in the most minute particles of the universe.

I picture these invisible particles that compose every piece of existence as having little dancing feet. Something as sturdy as a boulder does its own boulder dance but it also weaves in and out of the dance of the soil, the dance of the worm, the dance of the wolf. The stone, the soil, the worm, the wolf, cannot be contained. They dance with everything else that "is." What a marvel, to think that each cell of my body is part of an intricate interweaving of the dynamic life of creation!

These discoveries were revealed to me through workshops, conferences, and books on quantum physics, theology, spirituality, and holistic health, as well as literary pieces, including poetry. These teachers were building on the studies, insights, intuitions, and experiences of wise people of the past whose work I had read and relished, such as Teilhard de Chardin, William Wordsworth, Walt Whitman, Rachel Carson, and Emily Dickinson, who sensed the cosmic dance years earlier. I read and resonated with the current thought and explorations of Thomas Berry, Beatrice Bruteau, Fritof Capra, Annie Dillard, Elizabeth Dodson Grey, Joanna Macy, Mary Oliver, Sally McFague, Diarmuid O'Murchu, Elisabet Sahtouris, Rupert Sheldrake, Brian Swimme, Margaret Wheateley, Gary Zukav, and numerous others who were speaking a similar language while using a great diversity of images and literary styles.

No one person has been able to fully communicate this amazing dance of life to me, but Thomas Merton comes close with his description in *New Seeds of Contemplation*. Merton's use of the phrase "cosmic dance" set my heart singing. When I read it, I felt my early childhood experience of the inner dance being echoed and affirmed:

When we are alone on a starlit night; when by chance we see the migrating birds in autumn descending on a grove of junipers to rest and eat; when we see children in a moment when they are really children; when we know love in our own hearts; or when, like the Japanese poet Bashō we hear an old frog land in a quiet pond with a solitary splash—at such times the awakening, the turning inside out of all values, the "newness," the emptiness and the purity of vision that make themselves evident, provide a glimpse of the cosmic dance.[1]

There are so many ways in which the cosmic dance becomes evident. Space explorers discovered this oneness in a visual way as they marveled at the astounding beauty of our planet from 17,000 miles away. When they gazed at Earth sailing through space, they realized in a deeply profound way the power of its being "home" for all dwelling there. After Jacques-Yves Cousteau spoke with some of these space explorers, he commented: "From their exceptional journeys, they all came back with the revelation of beauty… They all emphasize that our planet is one, that borderlines are artificial, that humankind is one single community on board spaceship Earth."[2]

We simply cannot live apart from one

[1] *New Seeds of Contemplation*, Thomas Merton. New Directions Books, 1961, pp. 296-297.
[2] *The Home Planet*, ed. Kevin W. Kelley. Addison-Wesley Publ. Co., NY, 1988.

another. Our ecosystems are key reminders of this intricate ballet of interaction. One of the reasons our trees are such precious commodities is that they breathe for us. They give us the oxygen we need by purifying the air. Their roots absorb water and carry it to the leaves where it comes in contact with the carbon dioxide that we have exhaled and which the tree needs for its growth. (An acre of healthy trees can produce enough oxygen for eighteen people.) Forests also influence our lives by cooling and humidifying the air as the trees release moisture through their leaves and needles. We need trees and trees need us, it is as simple, and as marvelous, as that.

Those who spend significant time with the creatures of our planet also discover the power and beauty of the cosmic dance of oneness. Scientist Jane Goodall studied chimpanzees for almost forty years. A large portion of her life was spent in the Gombe wilderness of Tanzania. She sat in steaming sun and pouring rain, sometimes slept on the forest floor at night, as she watched for hours and hours. What she discovered was that "together the chimpanzees and the baboons and monkeys, the birds and insects, the teeming life of the vibrant forest, the stirrings of the never still waters of the great lake, and the uncountable stars and planets of the solar system formed one whole. All one, all part of the great mystery. And I was part of it, too.[3]

The soul of the world and our own souls intertwine and influence one another. There is one Great Being who enlivens the dance of our beautiful planet and everything that exists. The darkness of outer space, the greenness of our land and the blue of our seas, the breath of every human and creature, all are intimately united in a cosmic dance of oneness with the Creator's breath of love.

This book is about my experience of being with the cosmic dance, how I have fallen in love with Earth and how I have been enthralled with the mystery of Moon, Sun, and the Galaxies. It is a book about what I have learned from this great attraction to creation. My three discoveries have changed the way I look at everything and the way I relate to everyone. I see that I am not a separate entity, and never could be, because the tiny particles of my body are dancing, intermingling with the particles of life around me. It is not a matter of "them" and "me," whether this be people, rocks, sea anemones, clouds, or rabbits on the run. Rather, it is a matter of "us."

This "oneness" has challenged me to feel responsible and to care for our planet. When I used to hear facts about the termination of species, global warming, and destruction of rich farm lands and rain forests, I felt badly but did not think it affected me. I had absorbed the cultural lie that I was not con-

---

[3] *Reason for Hope: A Spiritual Journey*, Jane Goodall with Phillip Berman. Warner Books, NY, 1999.

nected to the land, creatures, sea, or air. As a human, I thought of myself as superior and separate from non-rational life. I never would have considered a prickly pear cactus or a wild whooping crane to have had a life interwoven with mine.

I now believe that few will feel the immediacy, pain, challenge, and tormented cry of our planet's devastation unless they sense a bond, an intimate link, with all that shapes and forms our planet. This is why it is vital to come into creation's presence with awareness, reverence, openness, and a humbleness that says, "I have much to learn from you. I am not better than you. We are simply different from one another."

Another challenge has also come my way from my three discoveries. It is easy for me to feel "one" with the stars on a shimmering summer night, to appreciate the dance in what appears good or in what appeals to me. It is quite another thing to feel "one" with an angry person or a poisonous snake. How difficult it is to see the inner dance in what repulses, divides, alienates, tests, or challenges me. I now understand that the cosmic dance is in destructive elements like tornadoes and earthquakes and in animals that destroy. It is also in the perpetrators of evil, in the hostile,

the violent, the aggressive, and in those who have maimed our planet by indifference, ignorance, or greed.

Yes, all are part of this vast dance of the cosmos and I am daily challenged to live compassionately with each person and particle of creation. It does not mean that I accept the reality of evil or harm. But it does challenge my ability to look deeply and keenly at certain aspects of creation in order to see an implicit relationship hidden beneath what I abhor or find difficult to accept.

Every day I am offered the tremendous gift of sipping from the mystery of life, tasting the exquisite beauty in what the universe offers me from the vast cup of the cosmos. And in the midst of this beauty, I am also invited to hear the groan of suffering that arises from our bleeding and wounded planet. It is my hope that this book of reflections on the cosmic dance will be a source of soul-tending and planet-tending for you. May it draw you to fuller enjoyment and appreciation of the mystery of life and its inherent goodness in yourself and in all of creation. In the words of Joanna Macy, may these reflections "embolden us to walk out into the world as into our own hearts."[4]

---

[4] *World as Lover, World as Self,* Joanna Macy. Paralax Press, 1991, p. x.

Chapter 1

THE DANCE

We Are One

little dancing feet full of energy
enlivening every particle of the universe,
tiny feet skipping, hopping, jumping,
strong feet stomping, jiggling, prancing,
leaping to a rhythm that defies regulation.

airy, bright feet of sailing stars,
wrinkled, callused feet of clay cliffs,
waxy, webbed feet of succulent leaves,
fast flowing feet of winding rivers,
endless feet of unobserved tree roots,
soft feet of every form of fetus.

with an eye as fresh and delicate as birth,
sneak a peek as each pulsing part of life
comes dancing, whirling, weaving,
secret neurons, veiled photons, hidden electrons,
whirling, skipping, pirouetting,
forming a circle of oneness with each other.

if your ear is keen enough, you will hear
their insistent, silent symphony,
moving freely in chasubles of beauty.

receive the music of their secret unity
as they glide within each other's life,
unaware of barriers built by static minds.

slip off the glaucoma of your heart
and revel in this signal beauty
dancing passionately
in the universe, and trembling in each atom.

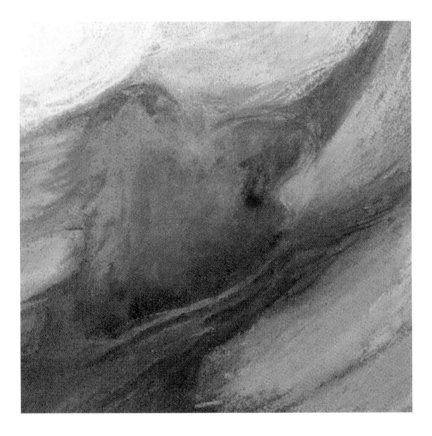

Energy is the substance of life,
the unrelenting wellspring of pure possibility,
escalating and undulating as in a great cosmic dance.
DIARMUID O'MURCHU

There is such power in the cosmic dance. Each time I resonate with this energy I sink into my soul and find a wide and wondrous connection with each part of my life. I come home to myself, feeling welcomed and restored to kinship with the vast treasures of Earth and Universe. I am re-balanced between hope and despair, slowed down in my greedy eagerness to accomplish and produce no matter the cost to my soul, beckoned to sip of the flavors of creation in order to nourish my depths.

When I was young, I presumed that each element of the universe was isolated from the other. My desk was a solid object and separate from me. The lilacs were separate from the garden fence. The cattle were separate from the fields in which they grazed. All was distinct, apart from the other. It was not until much later in life that I read the theories of great scientists such as Neils Bohr, Albert Einstein, Max Planck, Arthur Koestler, and others who developed the understanding that everything in existence consists of light and heat particles or waves that are constantly in motion.

These scientists referred to the light and heat of each piece of existence as packets of energy which were termed "quanta." It is these energy packets that are alive, interactive, and interrelated to one another, always moving, always involved in a constant dance of existence. They may look like they are self-contained in an animal, a human, a seashell, or a piece of metal but their patterns of movement can and do flow freely as in a dance. They can be changed and transformed by being in relationship to other particles of existence.

This patterned, or chaotic, movement of quanta is a mysterious process of motion in which there is constant change and interaction happening. Things are always in relationship to one another. One thing is affecting something else. Kentucky farmer and author Wendell Berry put it this way: "The world that environs us, that is around us, is also within us. We are also made of it; we eat, drink and breathe it; it is bone of our bone and flesh of our flesh."

The magic and the mystery of this cosmic

dance confirmed what I had sensed in my youth—that there was some sort of energy in what I experienced as the beauty and wonder of creation. This energy fed, nurtured, and resonated in my soul, wordlessly, giving me a sense of oneness with what I experienced. What I did not know is that this spiritual sense of being intimately connected to all of creation was also grounded in scientific discoveries.

Scientist Elizabet Sahtouris describes the beginnings of Earth in this amazing, interactive way:

Particles, or subatomic particles, are the tiniest whirling packets of pure energy from which all matter—all the stuff of the universe—is made. The whirling energy of particles created a new force, or forces, among particles, so that when early cosmic particles passed close enough to each other to attract each other, some of them held together as simple atoms. We can imagine this as rather like people dancing, attracting each other when close enough to whirl about each other...[1]

Many events and experiences lead me to glimpses of this marvelous cosmic dance. They are not necessarily "big moments." Oftentimes these glimpses are simple, quiet, unassuming ones. Usually they begin with the help of my five external senses. Maybe I am sitting in the park and I see a pair of robins perched on a thin mulberry branch, or walking

down a city street and a wild gust of wind sweeps by my face. Perhaps I stand still for a bit by a clump of trees, breathing in the freshness of the pines. I might be hurrying through a store and get caught up with the vulnerability of an elderly couple helping each other navigate through the crowds. It might be the simple gesture of sipping a cup of freshly brewed coffee or brushing rain off my coat. Each of these moments invites me into an awareness of the unspoken dance of energy connecting me to what I am experiencing. I sense for a moment that there is a hidden bond between myself and what is around me.

The cosmic dance is not limited to any one time or place. I have discovered it in the night sounds of the Liberian bush and in the crash of the magnificent waves against the cliffs of the southern Australian shore. I've sensed its power when walking amid the trees along the Black River in Northern Ireland and at the shrine of the goddess Kanon, south of Tokyo. I have beheld the dance in the laughter and cries of little children on airplanes and have seen it in married couples' eyes as they look with love and good humor. I have danced with this energy of life in celebrations and rituals with women's groups in many countries and alone on my hikes in the Rocky Mountains and while sitting in my own back yard.

I now truly believe that I can experience

---

[1] *Earthdance: Living Systems in Evolution*, Elizabet Sahtouris, iUniverse.com, Inc., 2000, p. 18.

this hidden dance everywhere, in a city full of tall buildings as well as in a small town where one can easily commune with trees and sky. I can know it whether I am driving on a busy expressway or down a narrow road past trim New England farms. Recognition of the cosmic dance happens in deliberate moments of contemplation but it also rises up surprisingly, like a breaching whale splashing high in the sea, commanding one's full and unexpected attention.

Wherever and however I join with the cosmic dance, it jogs my memory and gives me a kind of "second sight," a glimpse of the harmony and unity that is much deeper and stronger than the forces of any warring nation or individual. My trust that good shall endure is deepened. My joy of experiencing beauty is strengthened. My resolve to continually reach out beyond my own small walls is renewed. The energy that leaps and twirls in each part of existence commands my attention and draws me into a cosmic embrace. I sense again the limitless love that connects us all. I come home to that part of myself that savors kinship, births compassion, and welcomes tenderness. I re-discover that I am never alone. Always the dance joins me to what "is."

It Is Possible

it is possible
to become so one
with Earth
that every flower
perfumes the soul,

every snowflake
sends icy softness
dancing through veins,

every drop of rain
trickles down vessels
of the heart,

every cloud in the sky
sails along
songlines of the spirit,

every earthquake
rumbles in the gut,

every tide of the sea
moves in and out of self.

it is possible
to become one
with Earth

just as it is possible
to become one
with all people,
their pain, my pain,
their joy, my joy,
their struggle and delight
an echo of my own.

it is possible to become one.

it is possible.

The Mysterious Cosmic Dance

One day I sat and imagined some of the activity that might be taking place at that moment on the planet. In a few brief glimpses of my mind, I saw a hummingbird fly to a feeder, sipping red juices to her heart's content while, far away, a six pound infant entered the growing world of South Africa. A flabby seal off the Alaskan shores reached into the water for a walleye and in a corner of Hungary, a grandmother bid a final farewell to her family. A deer in British Columbia leapt across a green valley as the stars began to sparkle in the hushed silence of evening. A Japanese family gathered for dinner, lifting their chopsticks with satisfaction, while the red soil of Utah sighed with the touch of rain-drops reaching the thirsty land. Along the sultry Amazon, the humid air lulled crocodiles to sleep and in the distant South Pacific, aged volcanoes rumbled. Glaciers wept in Antarctica as they broke apart from their ancestors of ice, while descendants of Mayan Indians, wrinkled from long hours in the hot sun, worked their tiny patches of corn in Central America.

As I gathered these moments in my imagination, I felt a much needed stillness settle in my soul. The loneliness of past days departed with my awareness of the presence of others on the planet. The truth of each one's intrinsic vitality and vulnerability filled the hollow caverns of my heart with peacefulness. The strong sense of each one's being a part of a beautiful web and pattern of life soothed the sore edges of my spirit that were crying out for hope and communion. In those few moments I knew of my membership in a never-ending family. I stood up, breathed in the life-giving air of my sisters and brothers of the cosmos, and filled my lungs with confidence in our future.

Dance in the Sky

flickers of movement
in an early dusk sky,
long lines of activity
filling the horizon,

dancing they come,
the fast flying geese,
hearts bent on heading south.

no sound from their dance,
no chorus of conversation,
just swiftly moving wings
and an ever changing formation.

the lines curve and sway,
turn and re-form,
they half circle and straighten,
sweep out in fans,
come back again to singleness.

the dance of the geese
becomes a dance in my soul,
activity, movement, ease, joy,
a strong sense of purpose
and determined direction.

the dance in my soul,
may it be so, like the geese,
with great freedom of adventure
and sure hope of arrival.

Getting Inside the Skin of Creation

...listening to the rain falling I could hear the earth
distinctly speaking to it like a woman once more
in the lover's arms after a cruel separation.—LAURENS VANDERPOST

Sometimes I can get inside the skin of creation and feel the parched tongue of the dry vegetation. I listen to a gasp for moisture in the cornstalks that have browned from their ankles to their brows. I hear a death rattle in the leafy throats of trees. I feel the land's desire for rain, begging it to fill the rolling cracks on hills and the deep crevices of the dusty, furrowed fields.

When the gentle moisture finally falls from thundering clouds, I can feel it like a precious ointment as creation is rinsed and fed. I sense a peaceful resonance, a gentle gratitude, a taste of contentment. When rain soft as milkweed silk falls upon the waiting land, my inner tongue laps it up eagerly while I sit inside the aching cells of dried-out vegetation.

Sometimes as the precious moisture falls, I let myself become the raindrops as they are passionately welcomed by the dehydrated land. I sit beside the leaves laughing with wet delight. I plop in the puddles and fall deep into the heart of the furrows of tree bark. I weep in the raindrops as they turn into tears, sliding down the beaten, broken stems of wheat. I sigh as I fall into the withered hearts of lilies. I dance on the tight blooms of strawberries, teasing them toward openness.

Whenever I allow myself to get inside the skin of creation, I know I am in the embrace of Earth. I sense the vital essence, the dancing dynamism, and I bow to the One who holds this dance in an eternal embrace.

The Dance of Autumn Trees

This womb of trees
that I've sat under
all spring and summer
is feeling the death threats
of winter.

What amazes me
is that these trees
seem not to mind.

Could it be
a dance they are doing
in the wild wind?
Could it be a song
they are singing
through the raindrops
falling on their faces?

I cannot yet be
in the heart
of these autumn trees.

I am still
too much a stranger
to death,
too much a
clutcher
of the only life
I have ever known.

Eating Trees and Drinking Stars

When I was in Tucson, we had broccoli stalks for dinner. Helen said it was like eating trees. Indeed. They do look that way. And when I was in Colorado, Dorothy bought a bottle of champagne. As we sat sipping, she exclaimed that she was "drinking stars."

What is it about these two catchy phrases that leap like a little elf inside of me? They bring delight because they connect me with the planet and the universe. Yes, I am eating more than food and drinking more than liquid. I truly am eating trees and drinking stars. Everything is woven together in the loom of life. What feeds me has been fed by Earth. What I drink has been touched by stars. Sun has fed and nurtured grapes, those tiny beginnings of sparkle, as they matured and grew into ripeness. Moon has watched over them in the comforting shade of night, soothing these juicy fruits of vine with her tenderness.

Yes, I eat trees and I drink stars. It is a lovely thought, that one. I want to hold it near to me when I sit down to every meal. Bring on the broccoli and the champagne. It is time to hold hands with the dancing cosmos with every bite I eat and every sip I take.

The Old Closeness

The old closeness returned
last evening.
The solitude of dusk,
the beautiful gasp of sky,
the power of the full moon,
each one embraced me.

I sat in stillness,
held close in the cleavage
of evening,
resting my longing
on her gentle bosom.

Always in those moments
I am at peace,
freed from my bones,
at one with a home
far, far away,
yet eternally close.

Who said transfiguration
is only in the scriptures?
Who said we are only
what we can prove?

They are wrong
if they speak of such things.
Last night I could prove
nothing
but I knew
everything.

Chapter 2

AWARENESS

The Cosmic Tree of Life

I sank into the moist richness of Earth
and yielded to the softness of her breast.
I rested my ruminations in her embrace,
relaxed my hurry in her easy peace.

I closed my eyes and waited,
trusting in some faithful teaching.
At first I heard only the clashing jangle
of my overextended and anxious life,
but the longer I was attentive
the more I noticed the steady heartbeat
of something strong, deep, and true.

It was the cosmic tree of life singing,
rooted firmly in the crevice of my soul.

I saw in that moment of clarity
the ancient tree that never dies,
green and full of endless energy,
a central source of communion
fed by the tears of humanity,
nourished by the beauty of creation,
touched by the love of Eternal Oneness.

As the tree grew out of me, so did peace
rise sturdily within me, a pillar of love
breathing in, breath of all beings,
breathing out, love pure and undefiled.

And when I arose from my easy slumber
I looked to see that I had wings
inside of me,
wings as wide as the open sea,
wings as strong as the high flying eagle,
wings, silent, silky, soft as down
on the tender throat of a young sailing swan,

wings strong enough to cradle a universe,
yet gentle enough to nurture a newborn child.

At a certain point you say
to the woods, to the sea, to the mountains, the world,
Now I am ready.
Now I will stop and be wholly attentive.
You empty yourself and wait, listening...
ANNIE DILLARD

When I deliberately pause to look and listen to life around me I discover an amazing harmony within myself and all of creation. It is not always easy to stop, of course. I may be able to slow down my body, to sit relatively still in a lawn chair or at my desk. I may even lie down on the grass or lean against a tree or sit by the seashore. But even then, my mind and emotions can keep careening along, whirring at a dizzying speed due to my habitual pattern of constant activity and stress. I am too used to gobbling down my food, driving numbly through traffic, working feverishly while waiting for an appointment, thinking about tomorrow as I stand in line at the store.

There are times when my life rains a zillion details and I am so absorbed that I miss most everything and everyone. There are situations when I am so intent on being with someone in pain or so absorbed in my own hurt or sadness that I turn all my senses away, instead of toward what is happening to me and to life around me. There are moments when I am simply too weary and worn out to even care whether or not I am aware. There are other times when I am filled with judgment about someone or some thing and I miss the connections being offered to me.

No matter how pressed my life is or how fraught with difficulty, I do eventually wake up. My desire to be aware is restored most often through finally stopping, or being stopped, by the sheer magnificence of creation. I have been ambushed by the power of the moon, held captive by fireflies dancing at dusk, bowled over by wobbly white shoots beneath a rock pushing their way out to life, moved to tears by the sight of a small finch falling from the roof. I have lain on the picnic table and gazed at the stars in sheer ecstasy until I thought the only option for my heart was to die at that moment. I have sat still, stood attentively, hiked happily, skied freely, gardened with quiet vigor, and all with the intention of becoming more aware of life around and within me. When I have freed my spirit to become aware, I have never failed to find meaning and hope, gratitude and peace, comfort and encouragement.

If there is a lesson to be learned in all of this, it is that in busyness I often close down. In deliberate or unexpected awareness, I open up. It is in this openness that I "see" in a deeper or newer way, viewing people, creatures, and nature in a clearer light. As I open and become more aware, something happens inside of me to cause the barriers of my inattentiveness, judgments, or busyness to move aside and for bonding to occur. It is then that I recognize my oneness with the dancing that is inherent in the all of creation.

There are big moments of awareness but also many day to day ones that allow me to enter into this attentiveness. I do not need to be away from home or work in order to know this oneness. I do not need to be at the seashore or on a mountaintop to enjoy the cosmic dance. I only need to be awake and alert, to let go of my busyness and my self-absorption, in order to discover mystery and wonder in things like the food before me and the people at my side. There are stories of life dancing vividly on every level of the world in which I live. Each creature, person, cloud, city corner, rock, and plant has numerous layers of inner activity, threaded with meaning and circles of mystery, offering hope and encouragement to my life.

When I take a deep breath and pull in the reins of my "hurry" I begin to find the numinous everywhere. I notice the soft breeze and how it caresses, soothes, and quiets me. I look out the window beyond my desk and I see not just trees, I see how they behold the sun and receive the nurturance offered to them. I speak with someone on the phone and I hear not just a person's voice, but also the bond of life that connects us. I place my pen on the paper to write and I am lovingly united with the soil, rain, and sun that grew the tree along with the hands that labored to bring the pulp of the tree into the form of paper. In aware moments such as this, I see more clearly, lean into the mystery of life more deeply, and honor the oneness of life more truly.[1]

I learned how to be aware when I was young. I saw how my father would watch the skies for storms, how he sensed when it was the right time to plant and to harvest. He taught me how to sniff the air and smell the seasons, to look at winter skies and know when snow was about to land. I learned what hail clouds looked like in the spring and which clouds would bring the rain. It was Dad who talked about being able to hear the corn grow in the summer and who noticed how the maple leaves turned when a change was on its way. He was attentive to the farm animals and knew

---

[1] The Buddhist monk, Thich Nhat Hanh teaches awareness and uses the term "mindfulness." See *Thich Nhat Hanh: Essential Writings*. Orbis, Maryknoll NY, 2001.

when they needed special care. I watched him find the places where fish and turtles swam in local creeks and how he ran his hand through the grain as it filled the bins at harvest time.

Awareness was a great gift my father gave me. I did not know in those early years what a vital component of life I had learned. As I grew older I forgot how essential it is to be alert and attentive to what is a part of my life. It has taken me time to recover this gift and I still lose it now and again. I am growing in awareness, however, and each day I re-commit myself to this gift as I turn my entire being toward the cosmic dance, longing to lean into it with all I am and all I do.

This awareness is essential because my experience of the cosmic dance depends on whether my senses are alert and whether my heart is attuned to looking beyond what is visible. If I rely only on the rational, I will miss a good portion of the cosmic dance. If I fail to be still and to explore the far regions of mystery, the dance will remain aloof from my inner eye. Daily I must set out, again and again, to have an open mind and a compassionate heart. Daily I must perk up my external senses and commune with my internal ones, as well. The cosmos holds out her cup of life to me, filled with invisible packets of energy. I need only respond with a desire and an intention to receive. It is then that I enter into the cosmic dance with awareness and gratitude, and hear again the inner voice urging me toward oneness.

A Slip of Rain

Attentiveness is the natural prayer of the soul.
—Nicolas de Malebranche

A slip of rain, unexpected,
just enough to tickle the leaves
and encourage the flowers
to stick out their tongues.
Nothing more.

Thirsty blades of grass
barely feel the feathered moisture,
but my ears have heard
the whispering feet of raindrops
and my heart has felt the soft dance
of their gauzy landing.

I pause for a brief time
from my ballyhoo busyness
and enter the silvery silence.

So deeply enticed
is my parched soul
that I sit entranced,
unable to do anything
but listen.

I wonder if I will ever
get back
to my endless ego endeavors.

I wonder if it matters.

Playing Dead

A large, green grasshopper, jumping like he's in the circus, moves before me on the path. I step nearer and touch him with my long stem of grass. He's suddenly silent. Not a breath of movement from him, like a little bump of green. "Clever," I say to myself, "neat way of protection, this playing-dead thing."

I smile and move on, nearly squishing a slow moving form of yellow and brown stripes, a miniature porcupine, elongated of course. I stoop to touch this rolly form, anxious to feel the little brushes of color around the body. As I do so, the caterpillar quickly forms itself into one soft, curvy ball. No amount of teasing with my finger will cause it to unfold. I move it gently in all directions, and still no sign of life. "Clever," I say to myself, "neat way of protection, this playing-dead thing."

Then, I wander to the inside of my self, to the journey of my heart. I look at places where fears and old wounds keep me from being alive and fully a part of life. I see how maybe it's not so clever to keep on playing dead. Parts of me need to wake up, to be tickled in the ribs of my vulnerability by life's blade of grass. Parts of me need to jump high with delight, to leap along life's path instead of hiding out in the concrete havens of my overly protected self.

Too much of me is still "playing dead."

Secretly Sensed You Everywhere

He looked around him as if seeing the world for the first time.
The world was beautiful, strange and mysterious. Here was blue,
here was yellow, here was green, sky and river, woods and mountains,
all beautiful, all mysterious and enchanting, and in the midst of it, he,
Siddhartha, the awakened one, on the way to himself.

—Herman Hesse

I've secretly sensed you everywhere
in birch trees
in crystal clear lakes
in cool misty mornings
in rolling every-shade-of-green hills
in grazing-upon-grass animals
in early dusk drives into the city

in shaded walks
in sun sifting through ivy
in small silent flowers
in the dawns and the dusks
and the mid-afternoons between
the two and the rising moon

and now this
in laughing trees
in windows everywhere showing forest
in birds calling and cooing
for mates too far away to hear

I am caught now
in each

the vision
wraps a serene glow
around the tendrils
of my far-flung inattentiveness
and calls me home

Stillness

stillness

just stillness
like my world seldom knows.
inside I have an expressway
that never slows down,
always full of going somewhere
always another thing to do

stillness

just stillness
filled with quiet, numinous sounds,
like butterfly wings, river murmurs,
cloud breaths, firefly blinks,
and silence, simple, serene silence,
nothing more

stillness

just stillness
here in this satisfied space,
and I, so crippled from my chaos,
sound inside like the cawing crow
flying low over the pond,
breaking the stillness
with his harshly handled song

A Community in My Hand

One of the retreat processes I've facilitated and enjoyed is that of inviting participants to come to a greater awareness of what is in the present moment. When I was in Melbourne, Australia, I asked each participant to take a slice of apple, a raisin, and a grape. I invited them to ponder each piece of food, to first hold it, smell it, look at its color and shape, notice the texture and design, and then to eat it very slowly, chewing it many times before swallowing it. They then took the three pieces of food with them and went to their room, or outdoors, to fully enter into the experience.

Later when we re-gathered as a whole group I asked them what the process was like for them. One person said she forgot to eat slowly and just gobbled the three pieces of food down right away. Another said he was amazed at the taste of the fruit as he chewed slowly and savored the flavor. Others noted how astounded they were at the beauty of color and design which they had never noticed before. Many spoke of a feeling of gratitude that arose as they slowly ate the fruit.

One woman from a South Pacific island was very quiet during this discussion. As the retreat was drawing to a close the next day, I asked her how the retreat had been for her. Her eyes lit up as she gently spoke about the experience with the three pieces of fruit. She held out her hand, palm up, and said, "I had an amazing revelation. As I looked at the food in my hand, I realized I was holding a community! I thought of the people who planted the seeds and tended the fields, the ones who picked and brought the fruit to market, those who sold it and the ones who bought it there and prepared it for us to eat today. It was a profound moment for me to know that each of those little pieces of fruit was connecting me to such a large world."

Her comments left me in awe at what simple awareness can do. At another retreat some months later I told this story. Afterwards, a participant commented that she saw another community in the woman's hand as well: "The community of soil, rain, sun, air,—all that had helped to nurture the fruit." Her comment helped me to see an even fuller dimension of the cosmic connection within those little pieces of fruit. It is amazing to think that something so simple as those small elements of existence could have so much to say about our oneness with the cosmic community.

The First Time

imagine the first time
you opened your eyes
and saw a human face

imagine the first time
you touched your hands
and felt the softness

imagine the first time
you heard the sound
of your own name

imagine the first time
you looked at a flower
and smelled the fragrance

imagine the first time
you walked on your own
and didn't fall down

imagine the first time
you had a delicious bath,
warm and sudsy

imagine your first drink of water
your first ray of sunshine
your first time in a park
your first look at the moon

now take it all in again
as if today
is your last day...

Spellbound

walking quickly in the dawn,
frost tickling sleepy eyes,
thoughts all tangled
and squeezed with should
and ought and have to do,
when the sound of a hoot
lifts my awareness
into another layer of life.

flying she was, on the hill,
sailing through the trees,
wonderful to behold
as she landed on the dark branch
not far from where I stood,
spellbound by her presence.

all day yesterday
the vision of the owl
warmed my heart
and mellowed my work.

a barred owl it was,
deep dark eyes, spotted feathers,
exuding some kind of energy
that came to me with peace
and the markings of mystery.

today I looked eagerly for her
among the oak trees on the hill,
but she was nowhere to be found.

a chance meeting?
a planned encounter?
I do not know.
I only know that yesterday
stays long within my memory
and rests in me with ease.

Chapter 3
THE HEAVENS

Star-Breath

I lie awake on summer's greening grass
soon to be soft with evening's dew.
I lie expectantly, silently,
waiting for a presence to breathe upon me.

With the first sigh of the evening star
my heart responds to a distant touch,
a wisp of recognition, a waft of joy.

Life-giving breath of the galaxies
sails through the heavens
into my gasping, yearning spirit,
uniting me in the marrow of my soul.

Star-breath washes over me
like god-breath
filling the soul of a new creation,
awakening my soul's withered bones,
lifting them into lightness and dance.

I open my small, isolated self to the stars
and am once again healed of my disparity,
the falsehood of a separate identity.

Infusing star-breath fills my soul
with eternal oneness.
My being absorbs the star's sighing,
and I enter into the easy sleep
of endless communion.

There is a day, one day each year, when light from the rising sun strikes the peak of my childhood monastery in such a way that it looks, for a moment, as if it were lit from within. The very tip of its cone-shaped stupa glows like a torch in the sky. In those few moments, it shines with such radiance that everything stops to pay homage; the winds through the valley die down, the birds cease their song, and the families beginning to work in the fields fall silent. It lasts for only the blink of an eye, then it's gone. But its light, shining so pure, so bright, has stayed with me all these years. Ani Pachen

Through the ages people have been drawn to the lights of the heavens, not only because these lights comfort and guide in darkness but also because these vast twirling masses of light evoke a cosmic mystery. They stand as messengers of some limitless connection beyond human perception. Scientists continue to study, to perceive, to proclaim their theories, but in the last analysis, the vast orbs in the sky remain full of challenge and wonderment to mortals. The immensity of the galaxies, the power of sun to both create and destroy, the joy of a shooting star's brilliance, the possibility of falling meteorites, such things as these keep the human heart in awe and amazement.

It is in the heavens that the cosmic dance is most evident for it is here that we can see the patterns of the planets and the stars as they move in a mystic melody to the rhythm of the universe's song. In our own Milky Way Galaxy, Moon circles our Earth and other planets circle our Sun, each with its own regular and predictable dance. Out beyond there are trillions and trillions of dances taking place as each star sails with its own pattern of existence within the billions of galaxies in space, one and all creating exquisite dancing paths of light and heat.

Our planet Earth was once a dancing star, evolving over four and a half billion years ago from the many elements of a colliding supernova. I have loved knowing that we are "made of stardust" as Brian Swimme and other poetic cosmologists tell us.[1] I like knowing that the composition of my body has the elements of a star that was once brilliantly aglow in the universe and is now dancing in me. There's a magical sense of connection that comes from this knowledge: Stardust dancing in my bones.

---

[1] *The Hidden Heart of the Cosmos: Humanity and the New Story*, Brian Swimme. Orbis Books, Maryknoll NY, 1996.

Stardust leaping in my heart. Stardust doing a somersault in my brain. Stardust leapfrogging in my red and white blood cells. Stardust sailing through the layers of my skin. It is astounding indeed.

It is no wonder that I have been constantly drawn to the night sky, enthralled with the constellations, filled with glee at seeing a falling star. When I pause to be with the stars I sense a vast and eternal bond, a presence immensely kind and loving, yet also enticingly distant and intriguing. I am also drawn to the cycle of the moon with her light, soft and tender, and astounded by her power that dances the tides of seas across our planet.

Our sun is equally as attractive and compelling. It is easy to take the power and vitality of the sun for granted even though this immense source of energy is essential for existence on our planet. The movements of light at day's beginning and end are special messengers for me. The rising and setting of sun create my favorite times of reflection: dawn and dusk. These are the moments for me when there is a very "thin veil" between this life and another hidden one. It is easy to sense the dance within myself and the world beyond me at sunrise and sunset.

The seasons are likewise influenced and affected by light. Indigenous people throughout the planet studied the skies, knew the movement of the seasons, and could predict when the sun would be highest and lowest in the sky. Our ancestors celebrated the winter and summer solstices (sun's low and high times) with great vigor. Light in a non-electrical world was essential to their survival.

It is simply amazing to come to an ancient site like Newgrange in Ireland and see how carefully crafted it is. The sun at the winter solstice enters through a narrow slit aligned over the entrance of the tunnel leading into the tomb. This narrow slit catches the rays of the winter sun on December 21st and moves through the passage-way to illuminate the circular space for a brief seventeen minutes of time. I stood in the Newgrange site some years ago and as I did so, I felt an immense connection and oneness with the ancestors whose creative minds and hearts had known and expressed appreciation for the power and beauty of sunlight.

Clouds of all shapes, sizes, and color are also a part of the heavens. They are carried by wind and often slip in and out of the sky without our noticing. I have often found it difficult to befriend wild winds even though they, too, are part of the cosmic dance. Being small of stature, strong winds seem big and bossy to me. Gentle, soft winds are much easier for me to accept. Like all elements, strong winds need to be respected as sources of change in weather and in climate. There is no rain without the clouds, little shade without their shapes hiding us from the strong rays of the sun, no easing of a dangerous cold front without their warm breath. Strong winds also provide challenge and attention when they whistle up blizzards, dust storms, and intense hurricanes.

Wind circles our globe again and again, clearing out dull, toxic, lifeless air while bringing freshness and vigor. It has only been in recent years that I have become grateful to wind for drawing me closer to all people on the planet. Now I understand that the air I breathe is the same air, recycled through trees and plants, on the journey from other people and creatures in far away lands like Asia, Africa, and Australia. Again and again, wind circles around, uniting us all in the cosmic dance of the atmosphere.

As I stand in my own small space of the planet, reveling in the power and beauty of the heavens, I feel a great unity with all beings. I know that somewhere there is a herdsman in the Sahara Desert who is also gazing at the stars of our common universe. I know there is a lamb in New Zealand romping in sunlight that also bathes my skin. I know there is a woman in India who is going to sleep under the same moon I am. I know there is a cactus blooming in Mexico under the same sky as mine. I know that all of us are drinking in the wind and living under the beauty of the heavens. I know that all of this is a dance of oneness amid the bounty of the skies, and I am grateful.

Moonrise
on Penobscot Bay

she waits for no one,
this orange orb of wonder,
steadily climbing the silky sky
on an early September night

the stars bow to her,
gladly withdrawing their radiance
for this majestic rising
of potent beauty

she moves consistently higher,
her sparkling light flowing down,
brilliant rays of giant fireflies
dancing on the night sea

up, up, she climbs the sky,
so bright she awakens
the nestled wood creatures
stirring in their early dreams

I sit benumbed with splendor,
all thoughts and words
as if they never were,

waiting in vigil with this one
whose tender light reaches
the silent edges of my soul,
wooing me into eternity

Time to Wing Home on the Sunset

time to wing home on the sunset,

partridges shuffle in their nests,
settling in for the night.
geese honk farewell in the sky
their V-formation decidedly southward.

the wind gives way to quietness,
the full weathered walnut tree
sails golden leaves to an already
rich ground covered with goodbyes.

my heart hangs quietly by the small oak,
dark wine leaves stunningly bright
against the round red disk of the sun.

the deepest anchor of peace
settles inside my own nested heart,
and my feet seem unable to move.

for this is our time, Ever Present One,
our "you and me" time,
when all the world is benediction.
I meet you face to face,
veiled in the form of serenity,
winging homeward on the sunset.

Between Sun and Moon

Yesterday, in the freshness of dawn, I stood in the crisp air of early March and knew without question the splendor of my simple life. Dawn came in a strong way. No easy, slowly turning layers of pastel blues and peach hues. Rather, a huge red ball of fire rose majestically on the eastern horizon, announcing candidly that morning had arrived. One could hardly miss the vivid entrance.

Eventually, I did turn to continue my walk and it was then that I saw another large round ball in the morning sky. There in the blue space of the west was the full moon, still a bit high in the heavens before beginning the dip downward beyond the horizon. What a sight it was to see both of these magnificent celestial orbs of creation hanging there in the early morning sky!

I felt incredibly small, yet greatly privileged, as I gazed at those two brilliant lights suspended in the vast expanse: the yellow-orange fullness of setting Moon in the west and the red, pulsing fire of rising Sun in the east. As I stood between these two cosmic beauties, the dense body of Moon and the airy body of Sun, I felt an ancient cradling, an embrace of their two energies. I knew, then, with deepened clarity what it is to be a child of Earth, a daughter of Universe, a member of Cosmos. I felt protected, cherished, attended, by these two parents of the sky. I sensed I was being held within the arms of the Ancient One whose love was beckoning me to remember where I was before "now."

I stood with humility and wonder, held in the wide embrace, caring not about the day's schedule or the trivia of my desires. I rested for that moment in renewed peace, wrapped in the wide arms of Cosmic Beauty, convinced of a truth I can never explain.

The Darkness Settles

Strange, so it seems,
how darkness suddenly settles.
It hides in the light all day
then moves
with barely an eye blink
to casual de-lighting.

The darkness that settles
hides all lonely faces
and dirty, mud-lined houses.
It points out city lights
and candle warmth in windows.

The darkness that settles
tells the sky to have another moment,
gives birds a few fast swings of wing,
and hurries tired workers home.

The darkness that settles
marks the winter branches
as stringy streaks of black,
causes sun to hold its breath
so night can bless each moment.

The darkness that settles
brings a certain curtain freedom,
allowing each to hide
from what is fearsome in the light.

Thunderstorm

I awaken in the dark, muggy air of midnight, feeling glued to the pillow with all the moisture that is hanging in the summer air. In the far distance I hear the boisterous voice of the thunderstorm threatening to move in with destructive winds, sizzling lightning, and heavy rain for all those in its path. It crackles and rumbles with an ominous tone, slowly charging in like a train determined to meet its destination.

I arise in dread, unplug the computer, close the opened windows, and wait for the crashes of lightning and the huge booms of thunder to come closer and closer. Memories of storms on the farm come back to me vividly—the stories my mother told of how I was so frightened of storms as a child that they would often find me hiding under a rug, trembling with fear. I am a big girl now, I tell myself, and crawl back into bed instead of under it. I am not trembling but I feel fear, with its pointy, persistent feet, creep in around my heart.

The thunderstorm brews like a strong cup of coffee and while I cannot see the clouds in the darkness of night I imagine them to be just as thick and black. The rolling sound of windy clouds churns its way forward, a large, gruff voice warning all who are in its way that it can destroy and damage badly with one breath of its mighty voice.

By the time the loud-mouthed storm comes into the city, there is very little noise from the sky. A soft rain begins to fall in the dark silence. The rumbling moves on and nothing more ever happens. I lie in bed listening to the serene movement of raindrops on the leaves, wondering why I fear so much when the threatening noise is still at a great distance. I forget that thunderstorms are often like loud-mouthed people, rarely destroying their prey, just wanting to leave them shaking with fear to emphasize who's in charge.

So I turn on my side and ease myself into sleep again, determined not to get so fearful with the next rumbling storm. But somehow I know I will still have this urge to get up and hide under the rug when another thunderstorm comes charging in.

In Praise of Wondrous Sun

Sun! Fire from afar, unfailing source of radiance!

Your beams of bright light gift our planet with verve.
Juicy shoots of seeds rise up from their dormant death.
Fresh leaves uncurl, sipping in the dewdrops of dawn.
Forests open their arms to your shining shafts of light
and the winding ivy on trees blushes with your beauty.
Deserts sing with their hidden cache of flowering plants,
while your unabated beams dance in transparent design.

Your warmth dispels the darkness of the long winter.
Layers of ice melt and the frozen land thaws.
Human bodies are healed and dooming depressions lifted
by the purifying and nurturing rays of your light.

Clouds form patterns of brilliant color in early morning.
Shadows take shape in the heart of deep mountain valleys.
Faces of rocks and minerals sparkle with revelation.
Bird feathers shine with illuminating rays of your gold
and winding rivers glimmer with your reflected grandeur.

O radiant star! Source of nurturance, warmth, beauty!
Today I celebrate what you do for our life-filled planet
dancing 'round you, hour after hour, day after day,
sailing the cycle of life, season after season, year after year,
imbibing your shining rays with greening gusto.

Shine on, oh fire from afar, shine on!

Sky

I love the expansive sky over the mountains, valleys, canyons, and meadows. In my wooded home space with its canopy of trees, I rarely see sky in summer. Sky opens wide, offers freedom and expansion, reminds me of the largess of the universe. My trees are good companions. They keep me enclosed, focused, and offer cave-like attention. But how good it is to "get out and stretch" into a big sky, to behold a wideness that reaches into forever. Sky lets me see the constant movement of clouds and the dazzling patterns of the constellations. Sky holds mystery, so much beyond and unseen. It connects me to the universe, widens my perception and expands my sense of who I am in relation to "the world."

Swallows dipping low to catch mosquitoes, migrating pelicans, dark storms brewing, and breath-taking lightning bolts— all this I see with the gift of that wide open space. Sky is generous, allowing room for birds, kites, clouds, airplanes, stars, planets, satellites, space capsules, and much more. It is a vehicle for clarity, helping me see far and long. Sky is helpful, providing sources for me to find in which direction I am going and to reckon the time of day.

Sky is always available for gazing, offering a wide-screen view of sunrises and sunsets with glorious color. Sky transports essential moisture for the nourishment and refreshment of land and creatures. It holds the sun, a priceless energy for growth, warmth, and light. Sky carries winds, vital for cleansing air, changing weather patterns, and clearing out storms. Sky offers a home for planets and galaxies, gives them room to increase and change.

No matter where I stand on Earth there is sky, expansive, sweeping, wonderful sky!

Full Moon on Christmas Eve

The heavens are telling
the glory of God.

PS 19:1A

It is Christmas eve.
Small dry snowflakes
sing in the winter air,
a Gloria to late December.

Off we go to the country,
to my rural church
of long ago,
a choir of farming folk,
most of them quite old,
caroling from the heart
about the Babe of Bethlehem.

Their attempts at praise
bandaid my empty heart
amid a lifeless liturgy,
but what truly stirs my soul
is beyond the wooden walls.

Out in the Christmas sky
the full moon vigils,
filling snow-white cornfields
with an ethereal shine,
a steady gaze from the heavens
blessing Earth with simple beauty.

I travel in silence
among the sleepy talk,
longing to stop the car,
get out, dance awhile,
and fill my flat religion
with joy of another kind.

Chapter 4

EARTH

Gaia

When was the moment I fell in love with you,
nurturing and elegant mother?

Was it when fresh dew danced on the cheeks of ripened cherries,
or when the silent sentinel of Mt. Fuji smiled long at me?

Was it when I stooped down to admire little faces of pansies,
or when the perfume of lavender lilacs sailed into my soul?

Was it when I tasted the tomatoes from the vegetable garden,
or swallowed black raspberries from the wilderness bush?

Was it when I drank freely from an unpolluted stream,
or when I canoed across the clear water of Lake Caribou?

Was it when I swam with dolphins in the Atlantic's waves,
or when I listened to the steady laughter of a bubbling creek?

Was it when I looked in awe at the rainbow in Kauai's cleft,
or when I sat under the scrub oak listening to mountain rain?

Was it when I felt the first snowflake melt upon my eyelashes,
or when I walked aimlessly amid the musty autumn leaves?

When speaking about Earth in a personal way many refer to the Greek goddess
Gaia, who was formed out of chaos. From her body come the mountains, seas,
valleys, and sky. See *Earthdance* by Elizabet Sahtouris for a lovely description of
this process.

Was it when I planted daffodil bulbs and pressed them in black soil,
or when I touched the smoothness of an ancient stone?

O Gaia, each experience has drawn me to you,
one and all have anchored me in your beauty.

All of my days, replete with your bounty.

All of my life, a savoring of your elegance.

All of my nurturing, suckled from your sources.

All of my love, astounded at your goodness.

All of my journey, one great moment of unity.

Snow was heavy on the evergreens, but on the leafless twigs
it had been turned to glass. A lovely rosy glow enveloped
the whole landscape but the touch that made it unusual
and breath-taking was that every twig of glass was turned to amethyst
—do you wonder tears formed in my eyes?
RACHEL CARSON

Tears come easily when something of Earth's beauty surprises or astounds me. The inherent mystery and unspoken magnificence of the simplest things can move me deeply. It is humbling to experience Earth's treasures. In being so awed I realize what a gift it is that I could be privy to such loveliness.

The tears arise because of the intimacy inherent in the experience. At times Earth's beauty unites me with a presence that is as near as my own soul, yet enormously more expansive. It is as if, in that experience of recognition, I leave my "self" and travel into the beauty that is before me. At times like this, Earth draws my being toward the Great Being and invites me into the dynamic dance that is always in cosmic motion.

Long ago I fell in love with Earth and am deeply grateful for all I have come to know and experience of this incredible planet. Earth is a precious part of my life, a wonderful nurturing mother to me, always providing for my needs. Every day she offers me food to eat, air to breathe, and beauty to behold. I recreate in her parks, hike her mountains, and swim in her seas. I find delight in her colors, shapes, and sounds. I receive solace and renewal in her many forms of life. I discover teachings through her creatures and her seasons. No wonder I have a strong and enduring love for the many aspects of this immense and lovely globe of life.

I know this closeness to Earth is not true for all people. Annie Dillard, Earthy mystic, believes this appreciative relationship starts as a young child. This is true and yet it can also be cultivated as an adult. I know a woman who was in her fifties before she fell in love with hills and trees. There are others, though, who seem unable to have an intimate connection with Earth. I once heard someone say, to my great dismay, "Oh, if you've seen one mountain, you've seen them all."

It pains me to think anyone could miss the great diversity and variety that forms our planet. Just think of a few things that Earth is composed of: glaciers, hot springs, waterfalls, tinkling springs; caves, hollows, shady groves, wide forests; turf, sand, loam soil, clay, and stone; peninsulas, fjords, islands, flats, swamps; wilderness, desert, mesas, orchards, farmlands, bogs, paddies; savannas, meadows, plateaus, and plains; mountains, bluffs, valleys, ledges, cliffs, crevices; glens, harbors, lakes, rivers, creeks, and vast seas. To say nothing at all of the immense number and types of creatures that live on and within the treasure of this planet. Add to all of this the diverse textures plus colors of every shade and hue within the immense composition of Earth. To contemplate this for any length of time simply boggles my mind and races my heart.

There are many different kinds of places on our planet. These aspects of Earth influence and help to shape our psyches. We feel more at home in one place of Earth than another. I recall author Sam Keen saying, when he spoke in a Midwest city, that he could hardly stand all the green there. It was too much for him. He lived in the dried, brown land of western ranch country and felt alien in the rich, moist green farmland. My friend, Aileen, grew up on an island and took a ferry to school every day in New Zealand. She said she did not understand, at first, why she felt so terribly depressed when she went to live inland where the sea could not be seen. Another friend has never gotten over her homesickness for the white paper birch trees and the great waves of Lake Superior in northern Michigan.

Yet another relishes the energy and vibrancy of a large city. Some enjoy the endless sun of tropics or the frozen land of the north, while others are at peace among rainy days and fog.

I have lived most of my life on this planet in the Midwest where there are four very strong, distinct seasons. They have taught me many valuable lessons of life and I would miss them greatly if I lived elsewhere. Earth has brought me strength and courage through winter's endurance, hope and enthusiasm as spring awakens the land, gratitude and contentment in summer's fruitfulness, and wisdom from autumn's ability to let go and yield to dormancy and death.

My relationship with Earth continues to grow and strengthen as I make a deliberate effort to spend time with the many facets of our planet. Each day I go for a walk no matter what the weather and I eat outdoors as much as possible. In the wintertime houseplants keep me close to nature, as well as fresh flowers in a vase. When I travel I make a deliberate effort to notice the landscape wherever I may be. I pay attention to Earth through the vegetables, fruits, and other food items as I prepare a meal and through the water in a steaming bath or shower.

There have been situations where there was little nature to behold for a good portion of my day (a windowless office or conference hall, a stuffy meeting room …) but even then

I have been able to connect with Earth by noticing the food I eat and the water I drink. I've also used photos of nature on the covers of my journals and for bookmarks so that I am easily reminded of Earth's goodness.

As I have aged, it occurs to me that one of the most difficult things about dying will be leaving this amazing planet. The unknowns of the "beyond" do not bother me much. It's the "giving up" of this life so intertwined with the beauty and goodness of Earth that causes me concern. She claimed my heart long ago and I ache, even now, at the thought of never roaming her woods, walking by her rivers, touching her green, listening to the birds, feeling the sting of her sharp wind on my cheeks, looking at her soft, silent snowfalls, or catching a glimpse of deer or foxes at play. What joy can be beyond this side of life to equal what I have known here in beauty? I simply must trust—like the unborn babe who swims in the beauty of life within the womb—that beyond what I know here there is something else equally as beautiful and it will claim my heart as fully.

∞

A Small, Soft Feather

a small, soft feather,
still warm
from bluebird's wing,
falls onto the receptive
forest floor.

lightly it lands
under a thick-branched oak;
quietly it waits,
unnoticed, unattended,

until a sister of earth pauses,
beckoned by a flutter
of unseen energy.
she bows her kindled heart

stoops ever so slowly,
and the remnant of the blue bird
comes home
to her generous hand.

days later another earth sister
opens an envelope;
resting inside, waiting,
is the blue of sky
in shape of a feather.

from warm wing
to great oak,
to earth sister
to friend,
comes the soft blue signal,

and in a sparkle of recognition
a woman, weighed down
with too many wants,
remembers how to fly.

The Voice of Water

On an early Sunday evening in mid May three of us hiked to a waterfall in the Canadian Rockies. We stood in the fresh air, gazing at and listening to the unending water cascading down the long wall of boulders. As I stood there I noticed how the waterfall was unlike any others I had heard. It seemed to be a bit like a steady steam of broken glass. I thought, then, of how each water source has its own unique voice, much like humans do.

Water murmurs, sings and sighs, croons, gurgles, glups and glugs, pulses, splashes, laughs and cries. Some of these voices demand my attention while others provide just enough background music to ease the strain of a worried heart. Sometimes the voice of water has a rhythm of peace like the lullaby of a gently winding river. At other times, it holds the passionate energy of a booming mountain creek carrying tons of melted snow down its thundering path.

The tinkling of a tiny rivulet flowing from a secret spring tucked away in the heather has brought me joy, as well as the chattering voice of a bubbling brook meandering through a meadow. I've felt cautious as I listened to the raucous splashing of rapids and awed at the hollow stillness of a stagnant pool in a dark forest. I've heard the huge cracking cry of glaciers as they dropped to death into the sea, strained to hear the barely audible murmur of a farm brook going dry. One of the most tender voices of water I've heard is that of melting snow sifting through brilliantly green moss on a stone ledge, falling onto wintered humus below.

Some voices of water calm me like the tap, tap, tap of raindrops on elderberry leaves or the steady downpour falling onto city streets. Other voices call me to attention like gushing water out of the rain-spout, the persistent plop, plop, plop of heavy morning fog forming icy edges on the street signs, and the thin voice of snow as it begins running in rivulets on the window ledge. There are also certain voices of water that irritate me like the drip, drip, drip of a leaking faucet, the steady swish, swish, swish of the lawn sprinkler and the sloshing voice of water when boots drag through it.

Waves of water have their own special voices: the rough water behind a speedboat, the steady swish and swoosh of the sea's ebb and flow, the easy whisper of a great lake when water laps the shore, the pounding waves upon the beach on a stormy day, and the gravelly voice of the sea rolling over rounded stones like a can of shaken marbles.

There is the soothing sound of water in a baptismal font as it seals a sacred life, the refreshing voice of water poured over ice cubes on a hot summer day, the sighing of steaming water as it rests in the bathtub, and the dashing voice of water in the morning shower.

Oh, there are so many voices of water!

Nasturtiums

nasturtiums,
wrinkled round bits
of dry potential.
I pick them out,
one by one,
from the seed packet
and push them gently
into the moist, dark earth.

my polished fingernails
are laden with dirt
and I wonder if, like Enki,[1]
little creatures
will spring to life.

Even now as I dig,
and push, and cover the seeds,
something in the moment
begins to dance.

it is the secret
in the seeds,
it is the smile
of the rich soil,
eager to welcome
the silent daughter
of hope,
hidden in little
nasturtium seeds.

[1] Enki is the god who helped the Sumerian goddess Inanna escape from the Underworld by creating little creatures out of dirt so they could slip through the gates of the Underworld unnoticed.

Approaching a Stone

I learned a powerful lesson from Eagle Cruz, a Yaqui native, who had spent most of his life with the Plains Indians. One day he brought two huge stones to class and plunked them down in the middle of our circle. He called them "Grandfather" and "Grandmother," then proceeded to teach us how to approach a stone before we used it in any way.

He told us that stones are the oldest elements on Earth. They carry memories of cosmic explosions and journeys in space. They hold stories of Earth's origin and of the development of our planet. While stones can very slowly dissolve and erode, they are by far the most faithful and enduring of all the inhabitants of our planet. Small wonder that Eagle Cruz referred to stones as our revered ancestors.

So how does one approach a stone that has as much right to be here on Earth as humans do? Just as one would approach a person they wanted to get to know: slowly, carefully, respectfully, invitingly. We don't get to know a stranger in a minute or two and neither do we a stone. We need to stand and gaze upon the stone. Notice its qualities. Study its shape and color. Be with it. Then we walk slowly toward the stone, asking permission to sit on it or to pick it up. And most certainly, if we plan to take it with us, we must invite it to come along to a new home.

I was aware of this teaching of Eagle Cruz many years later when I was swimming in a clear lake not far from the boundary waters of Minnesota. I needed some stones to keep my mosquito netting from being blown away. As I lifted each stone from the water I gave thanks to the stone and promised to return it to the lake when I was ready to leave. This simple gesture gave me a special bond with the stones all week. Gratitude arose in me each time I took notice of them.

Some would say "oh, that's just ridiculous" when they read of stones, rivers, soil, or other "inanimate objects" having a dynamic life of their own, of their exuding an energy that interacts with us and with all of life. Yet, if quantum theory is true—that every particle in the universe is composed of an energy that pulses and interacts with other parts of life—then each thing of Earth has its own particular dynamism. Even a stone.

Winter Solstice

did I hear a groan today,
or was it the ancient sigh
of Earth turning slowly
in her frozen winter bed,
a momentary yawning
before she re-enters sleep,
snoring through the months
'til warm breezes stir her blood?

an easy stillness
sings beneath the snow,
a canticle of acceptance
plays upon the harp of frost,
wind lullabyes terminal buds,
while seeds of a past season
lay locked in the deep slumber
of a hushed and waiting soil.

my heart understands this season
and lately has learned to respond.
she, too, climbs inside the cave,
nestles close to silent seeds.
she, too, presses her check
to the hibernating dark
while she dreams of transformation.

Trees Teach Me

Whenever I spend time with a tree there's always a teaching to help me with whatever is calling me to grow. Sometimes there is nothing in particular stirring in my life, but being with a tree will release a thought in me that serves me well at a future time. I lean against, lie down under, and stand by trees. I ponder them from my office window and hold hands with them when I pause to touch their branches in the park. My life would be bereft if I did not have a tree or two to keep me company and to teach me things I need to know.

I've learned how to not be broken from life's unwanted things by watching a willow in the wild wind tossing and bending rather than pushing back against the storm. It's taught me that I can't always have everything go my way. Sometimes I need to bend a bit.

Paper birches have reminded me to surrender as their bark peeled off to aid the growth. The ponderosa pines of Colorado have urged me to be resilient as they stood sturdily through the turbulent mountain seasons. Enduring cottonwoods, with their many fibrous roots, have counseled me to sink strong webbing roots of love and faith so I will still be nourished in dry times when I question most everyone and everything.

Old dead trees in the moist woods persuaded me that life can come through death as

their decaying bodies nurture soil and seeds. The sycamore's round terminal buds on leafless branches showed me how to wait patiently through the dormant times of my inner winters when all seemed unable and unworthy of growth.

Trees have taught me about hospitality as I've seen them housing animals and birds. The live oaks of Louisiana prompted me to be compassionate as they shaded and protected me with their wide reaching arms. I've learned about unity and community from clumps of aspen groves and poplar shoots that nurture one another.

Fruit and nut trees of all types and tastes have influenced me to give away freely of my work and talents as I saw their bounty harvested for market. The thorns of the honey locust warned me of the price to be paid for the sweet pulp within its twisting pods, not unlike the challenge in the price I once paid amid the thorns of a challenging, yet successful job.

A new green shoot growing from a maple stump assured me that new life can come despite my woundedness, and the mighty redwoods have advised me that aging can be a graceful process with an inherent dignity.

On and on the teachings go. They never end. Not as long as I listen to the trees.

Chapter 5

CREATURES

Kinship with Creatures

Give praise to the Beloved,
all the earth,
all that swim in the deep,
And all the winged ones of the air!

Give praise all mountains and hills,
all trees and all minerals!
Give praise all four-leggeds
and all that creep on the ground!

Ps 148 (Nan C. Merrill, trans.)

Insects, birds, mammals, mollusks, and more,
my sisters and brothers, living beings,
each of us seeded in Earth's sacred womb.

We drink from the same running waters,
find nourishment from the same sun-fed soil,
unique cells dancing and tumbling in form,
separate yet connected, declaring we are one.

I applaud the bull snake's brave shedding of skin,
cheer the sand cranes dancing their mating games,
laugh with the kookaburra singing her song,
walk at dawn near young foxes leaping with life,
warn mosquitoes to keep away from my skin,
admire busy spiders spinning intricate webs,
listen to singing locusts and frogs harmonizing.

I stroll in the park with butterflies and bees,
work in the garden with ladybugs and moles.
I wear sheep's wool, drink cow's milk,
enjoy the omelets of eggs and pour
the fruit of bee's hard work into my tea.

Heard, or unheard, their melody is near.
Seen, or unseen, creatures are with me
as we sleep in the same great arms of Earth,
and sip from the same large river of life.

*The fifth kingdom is that of the animals,
multicellular heterotrophs with developed capacities for digestion. The largest subgroup
of those classified is that of the insects, some eight hundred and fifty thousand species. There
are at least five hundred thousand species of round worms and forty thousand vertebrate
species. Among the vertebrates there are nine thousand bird species, six thousand reptile
species, and four thousand five hundred mammalian species.*

Brian Swimme & Thomas Berry, *The Universe Story*

*I*magine all the creatures that have lived on Earth since the beginning of time, both those now extinct as well as those whose life forms still dance on the planet. The diversity and variety of creatures on land and in the sea is astounding. My experience of the beauty, wildness, instinctual wisdom, compassion, humor, cleverness, and freedom of creatures has enriched my life with kinship and companionship beyond measure.

Humans throughout the ages have been fascinated with the creatures of our planet. Historic sites like the limestone cliffs in southern France contain paintings and drawings of bison, rhinos, leopards, bears, oxen, lions, horses, and other creatures that existed during the Ice Age over 35,000 years ago.

My earliest recollection of a creature I felt kin to was our farm dog, Pal, a large friendly collie. I loved Pal and hurt for him when he would whine and moan with the noise of thunderstorms that pained his sensitive ears. Pal was a loving playmate, letting me ride on his back when I was little, and was always very protective.

Creatures are beautiful. I will never forget the hundreds of starfish that came in with the tide on Elephant Island, south of Anchorage. As I waited for the tide to return them to the sea, I was astounded at the great variety of colors and sizes of the starfish with their stippled and striped designs. I felt like Alice in Wonderland walking among those gifts of the deep with their bright orange, pink, green, blue, yellow, and purple bodies.

I am especially enthralled with creatures in the wild. Their presence unglues my little world of control and lets me breathe in the beauty and freedom of their untamed presence. Watching herds of rutting elk thundering out of the forest at dusk in Colorado, sighting a black bear in a ponderosa pine tree, hearing coyote yips in the night, coming across moose munching away in a marsh in Maine, kayaking with sea otters by my side and porpoises at play in the sea, hearing the swish-swish of fruit bats over my tent, sighting an emu in the tall grass of Australia, all these have been marvelous moments for me.

Creatures have brought me laughter and admiration of their astute and clever traits. One night I went to the porch and saw a large raccoon standing on his tiptoes pulling the bird feeder down on the branch, sucking out the seeds. I shooed the raccoon away and raised the feeder higher. The next night I looked out and saw the same raccoon standing on tiptoes, again eating from the feeder. Up above him was another raccoon holding down the branch for him!

Creatures can be very compassionate. Elephants mourn the death of their own. Certain horses are known to have intuitive skills whose presence is healing for humans with pain. Some dogs and cats are attached to their owners and often enter a grief-like depression when a beloved owner dies. There are numerous situations where dogs give their lives for their owners or sit by their sickbeds, never leaving their side. A bat was described in the *National Geographic* as "being a midwife" to another bat who did not know how to give birth. The pregnant bat was hanging upside down and the other bat came beside her and demonstrated how to hang upwards so the baby could slip out.

Female creatures have immense mothering qualities. In a terrifying death experience, a bird caught in the Yellowstone Park fire was found petrified in the ashes, perched at the bottom of a tree where she had instinctively gone to try to save her babies. When the ranger moved the dead bird with a stick, he found three tiny chicks still alive under their dead mother's wings.

Sometimes I have to face my fear when entering a creature's world, like hiking in areas where there are mountain lions and bears, or like the day I walked on a trail in northern Minnesota and a hawk, protecting the nest of a newborn, dive-bombed me again and again. (I had never had such big wings whoosh so close to my head!) Or the time a kangaroo came out of the bush, fulfilling my wish to see just such a one. I coaxed him near to me and then he came too close for comfort, sniffing me from foot to head, even touching my cheek with his mouth. I held my breath, wondering if he intended to bite me, but he was just a very curious creature.

Not all creatures I've known have been far from home. Equal delight and teachings have come to me from those in my own back yard and down the street. I have touched a newly born fawn sleeping on the side of a bike path, watched the amazing movement of garter snakes, found comfort from a hoot owl, listened to geese honking in the sky, discovered a possum in a bush by the porch, sat long watching a squirrel gathering dry leaves in his mouth as he made his winter nest, had monarch butterflies sit on my head and spiders spin insistent webs in my house.

I admire the resiliency and inherent wisdom of creatures. The golden plover flies 8,000 miles from Argentina to nest and hatch her young in northern Canada. The caribou have only 3 months to eat enough vegetation to last them through the rest of the year and the female caribou knows that she needs not only green grass and leaves, but also tree bark which provides calcium for her calf.

Migratory creatures teach me that what I need for my life is deep within me if only I will listen. Each season Pacific salmon search for the stream of their birth. They swim intensely until they reach that place where they spawn and begin new life before they die.

Monarch butterflies go to central Mexico each winter, going through several generations of dying and birthing before they once again reach their northern home in the spring. Honeybees find their way back to the hive and ants to the hill. Loggerhead turtles crawl away from sand dunes where they are born and swim directly toward an ocean they have never seen before. The little blackpoll warbler flies from its home in Nova Scotia to South America and manages to come back home again.

Creatures are simply amazing. I feel humbled by their courage and their wisdom. How glad I am for the oneness I have with them.

The Quail

we came upon them
on a high, wooded hillside.

with intense swiftness
they lifted up and out
of their hidden homes
in the tall browning grass
and were gone.

a swift flapping of wings,
a brief glimpse
of small, plump brown bodies,
that was all.

my heart caught a beat
as they surprised us
with our surprise upon them.

neither the birds nor we had time
to say hello.
we never gave each other
a chance to get acquainted.

we might have liked each other
but fear fed the flight
and we never touched.

Bush Berries

it is the time of berries on the bush,
colorful clusters of dark purple,
bright red, orange, burgundy, yellow,
fully ripened and ready to be gathered.

bears come down to the lower elevations
feasting and filling at autumn's table,
eating berries to their belly's content,
readying for winter's meager season.

I walk by the bushes in a world of beauty,
my soul singing in tune with Earth,
crisp, cool wind rides the wide valley,
clumps of red, cone-shaped sumac smile.

as I walk, I wonder if the memory
of colorful bush berries in September
will sustain my soul in the dark days
of winter's great intrusion.

will memories of the good times
erase the harsh edges
of life's unforeseen afflictions?
I do not know, but I hope it to be so.

thus I continue to gather memories
of my soul's rich, contented times,
much like a bear devouring bush berries
before the winter's heavy snow.

Wildebeests

Creatures are always teaching me. On one television program I learned that certain animals have an astounding ability to survive in very harsh conditions. Among these are wildebeests, who manage to not only live in the severe droughts of the African desert but to also give birth in those challenging circumstances.

I watched as a pregnant wildebeest, ready to give birth, stood up and easily let her newborn fall out of her. The little one wriggled loose from the placenta, stood up almost immediately, wobbled, fell, stood, wobbled, fell, and then stood up solidly on her thin little legs. She went right away to the mother's udder and began to take in nourishment because, as the commentator noted, within five minutes after birth the young wildebeest needs to be ready to run with the herd in order to be safe from predators.

At the same time that the little wildebeest was birthing and feeding, all of the female wildebeests formed a protective circle around the newborn, constantly watching for any danger that might be present. Then within a short space of time, the entire herd took off running across the vast desert.

As I watched this astounding process I thought of my inner birthings and wished they had more wildebeest in them. It seems that I often wobble and fall, stand up, wobble and fall, for quite a long time when something new is being birthed in my life. I get impatient, then ease up on my expectations, get scared, then face my fears, doubt my abilities and then trust my growth, wobble and fall, stand up shakily, wobble and fall … you get the picture. As this process of inner birthing goes on, I know that I must also nourish my inner spirit, just as the newborn wildebeest quickly realizes he or she must find strengthening food.

Like the wildebeests, I need the strengthening presence of others in my vulnerability. They can protect me from predators that would keep me from my inner birthing. These enemies are mainly the voices within me that deter me from my growth, voices that suggest my birthing is not worth the energy it takes, or that I've not the courage, or strength, or skill to do it. Circling around me are all those who offer me their compassion, understanding, comfort, patience, and encouragement as I struggle to change and to grow more fully into my true self.

I'm grateful for the strength of the wildebeests who have been around me in my birthing times. They have helped me to be up and running with the herd, moving through life with a truer awareness and acceptance of my best self. Because of them, I am also more trusting and more confident that loving communion is possible, that it is already seeded in those unseen energy packets of life that dance within each one of us.

A Trilogy of Insects

I. Spider

I tossed him out of my house
gently but with determination,
told him not to return again:
"This is my home, not yours.
Stay outdoors where you belong."
Later I went into his space
not thinking of my earlier dismissal.
His vengeful bite not noticed
until my chewed skin began to swell.
Even spiders nurse their grudges.

II. Night Visitors

All night while I slept soundly
I unknowingly shared my space
with three other creatures of God.
A June bug snuggled into my living room rug,
a centipede snored on the bathroom wall,
and a clear-bodied spider bedded in the pantry.
We all enjoyed a good night's sleep
and shared our mutual space in peace.
Why then, when I awoke to the light,
did I hurry them all outside?
No different were they in the daylight
than they had been at midnight.
What fearful voice in my psyche
suddenly found them unfit guests?

III. Walking Stick

You hang there on the patio table
with your quiet brown legs,
no more than a twig with eyes.
My friend, my best friend,
calls me to come, take a look.
Together we lean over and peer
at you, fragile piece of creation,
silent messenger of stillness.
And we both wonder to each other
why you have come to pay us a visit.
Could it be our restless spirits
needed your motionless reminder?

The Winter Dance

She climbed out of the comfort
of old grandmother Ryan's quilt,
and softly padded her way
to the frosty wintered window.
There she stood for one last,
lingering goodnight look.

Darkness had lain long already,
the moon high in the sky,
layers of ice sealed the land,
snow filled the wooded hills.

Faint murmuring memories
of summer's greening stirred
as she looked at the forest path.
Little snippets of desired warmth
teased her attentive heart.
Thoughts of verdant abundance smiled
in the corner of her gathered dreams.

As quickly as they had come
these memories of greening times
flew to their cloistered closets,
replaced by an enchanted scene
in the glen beyond her house.

Foxes with thick January coats
leapt into her windowed view,
chasing each other's red tails,
running, darting, skidding,
sliding on the ice, careening
around rough-barked tree trunks,
dancing, yes, dancing, in the night.

She stood long, looking in awe
at that marvelous sight
through the frosted window pane.
Finally, she went from there
to slip beneath the ancestral quilt,
wrapped in the happiness of Earth,
comforted by some unseen scent
rising like the rapture of red foxes
cavorting in a wintered night.

The Beauty of Birds

*B*irds carry such mystery within them. A gum tree full of chatty white cockatoos, great winged cranes flying over the Platte River, tiny hummingbirds sipping from red petunias, a vulture sitting and sunning itself with wings spread wide, loons calling to one another on the lake. What secrets lie within these creatures? What inner stirring urges their flight through the corridors of the sky? Why do they decide to nest in certain places? How do they know to teach their young ones to fly?

How different my world would be without bird songs. I marvel at the melodies playing through them. The brilliant red cardinal's crisp call is my morning alarm clock. The chirps of finches and the tat-a-tat of a downy woodpecker greet me in the garden. The nuthatch skips upside down along the maple branch with his rattly chortle. It is a beautiful symphony for my ears.

It is easy for me to identify with the diverse characteristics of these winged creatures. Some days I am a mockingbird filled with songs, diverse and strong, floating with creative zeal. Other days I am the crow, with one boring, endless call, circling around unceasingly. Yet other days I am a focused hawk or a squabbly blue-jay. On certain days, I feel I contain the beauty of the swan and other times, I feel more like the gangly, untidy heron standing in the muddy swamp.

Even more than their songs and their freedom of flight, I am consistently touched by the migratory instinct of birds and the pattern of their formations enroute to their destination. One September a gorgeous flock of pelicans flew over me. As they gathered for their journey south, they performed an air show, their black tipped wings and white bodies v-ing, circling, spreading out in a spectacular kaleidoscope. When they turned in the sun, there was a wave of darkness and with another turn, a dazzling white, depending on whether the wings or the bodies leaned into the light.

Each time I hear the honking of geese on their flight to some distant land, my heart skips a beat. Part of my spirit longs to ride on the wind with those fast flying ones. I look at their constantly changing formations and wonder at their strength and wisdom in traversing the sky so magnificently. Something in me yearns for their strong sense of direction and destination and envies the community they share in their journey.

Some scientists believe migratory birds follow magnetic energy patterns of the earth. It may be somewhat like the indigenous people of Australia following their own song lines of the land as they travel. I only know that something strong draws the birds into their journey. Some ancient story passed down from one generation of birds to another rests in their souls and nudges them intuitively into flight when it is time. Perhaps the songs they sing as they travel are the memories of their ancestors and the skies they crossed. Or it may just be that they are singing to the Great Winged One who guides all our destinations.

Creatures of the Pond

I circled slowly around the pond,
the full moon of early June rising,
greeting me as I followed the path
around the misty, shimmering water.

It was a night filled with sound,
bullfrogs, peepers, treetoads,
and crickets of all sorts and sizes,
castanet voices trilling the air,
night creatures of the pond
serenading with a loud lullaby.

Their night song drew me in,
cradled me in creature-calls rich
as foghorns in a milky-evening sea,
steady as violins with one long note.

I walked for a long while
where those creatures of the pond
were abounding with life,
where the darkness gave them voice,

and for that space of summer night
my empty heart, full of grief,
took comfort in their steady song,
assuring me that the dark night inside
might also contain an embracing melody,
if I walked slowly all around it.

Chapter 6

PEOPLE

A Piece of Light

As the sun rose, it filled me until I thought I was all light
and there was nothing left of what I once called ME.
Then suddenly I saw below at the water's edge
another sister of light. My light streamed out to her.
Her light flowed back to me and we were one in the light.

—MACRINA WIEDERKEHR

There is a piece of light in all of us,
easily seen in the wise Thomas Berry
longing to heal the wounds of our planet,
in Dorothy Day who embraced the poor,
and Mahatma Gandhi, fighting for peace
with the weapon of nonviolence.

There is a piece of light in all of us,
the grandmothers and grandfathers,
children orphaned by AIDS and war,
the feeble, the lame, the disheartened,
the successful as well as the searcher.

There is a piece of light in all of us,
maybe hidden or buried with pain,
perhaps pushed in the corner by shame.
It is there in the arrogant, the hateful,
racists, torturers, and abusers,
and ones who are willing to kill.

Seen or unseen, the light is there,
ready to kindle, eager to expand,
refusing to be tightly contained.
As soon as the tiniest space is allowed
it quickly emerges, floods outward,
illuminating the darkest of places.

One single candle lights a little dark space.
Many candles light a world full of people
desperately in need of each other's glow.

Each lone light makes us stronger
when we all stand together.

. . . not only was Christ in every one of them, living in them, dying in them, rejoicing in them, sorrowing in them—but because He was in them, and because they were here, the whole world was here too, here in this underground train; not only the world as it was at that moment, not only all the people in all the countries of the world, but all those people who had lived in the past, and all those yet to come.

CARYLL HOUSELANDER

The beauty and variety of people consistently bring joy and challenge to my life. All I need do is to sit in a busy airport for a few hours to know there are people of all sizes, shapes, and skin color, filled with diverse philosophies and values. One thing I have felt confident about for a good portion of my life is that it is mainly on the surface that we are different. We are not nearly as separate as we sometimes feel ourselves to be. Underneath our supposed differences we experience many similar emotions, longings, hopes, and dreams. The cosmic dance goes on in each and every one. It is the externals of appearance and behavior that divert our attention from the inner radiance and dynamic goodness within every being.

I was on the tram in the Dallas airport one day and all of us were standing or sitting quietly, avoiding eye contact and conversation with one another. Then an elderly man who was holding his wife's hand spoke. He told us they were traveling to celebrate the birthday of a special granddaughter. One person wished them well, then another spoke about it being her 40th birthday that very day. Many "happy birthdays" rang through the air. Soon we were all caught up in the conversation, laughing and enjoying the moment. As the tram came to a stop I realized that in our brief space of time we had discovered our oneness. As we stepped off the tram, however, we all pretended once again that we were isolated individuals and hurried away to catch our flights.

Another time that a stranger led me back to my oneness with humanity was while bathing in the hot springs south of Tokyo. While I sat there seeping in the comfort of the soothing waters, a thin, wrinkled, elderly Japanese woman continually looked at me with an intent curiosity. Later, when we had both emerged and dressed, I sat in a chair waiting for my companions. Quietly this same woman came up to me with a little smile. In her delicate hand she held out a tangerine for me. I smiled in return and opened my hand to receive the gift. In that gesture of giving and receiving, I felt a leap of kindness and respect between two human beings, younger and older, joining opposite worlds of East and West. In that gesture of kindness all dualism faded, dissolved. What remained strong and true was the dance of a Great Love uniting us.

Both Thomas Merton and Caryll Houselander had moments of glimpsing the true oneness of humanity. Merton was standing on a street corner in Louisville, Kentucky, when he suddenly saw the people surrounding him as a great body of life. He felt deeply and intimately connected with them in a vast oneness of spirit. A similar thing happened when the writer and artist Caryll Houselander was traveling on a crowded underground train in London. She looked around her and in her mind's eye she saw the Christ in all of them. But she saw even more than that. She had a profound sense that she was one with every person who had ever lived and ever would live, that there was an immense bond between them because of their mutual existence in time and eternity.

There are many ways to speak of the oneness that people have with all of humankind. Scientists describe this communion as the comingling and dancing of atoms one with another in people who are formed of the same stardust, breathe the same recycled air, and drink from the same streams of life. Christian theologians present this oneness as humanity's participation in the Body of Christ. Buddhists speak of it as the practice of compassion which

views all beings as one. Native Americans approach this same oneness in their understanding of each person as their brother or sister.

Modern writers refer to this oneness as the global village. Communication today happens with amazing speed and clarity in spite of the differences in language and custom. It is less and less possible to live as isolated human beings on our planet. Yet the differences among people continue to bring division rather than harmony, to produce domination struggles and war rather than enrichment, strength, and peacefulness.

People have influenced my experience of life in many ways. They have brought me joy and gratitude, challenged my beliefs and attitudes, stretched me toward growth, and strengthened me by their welcoming presence. I close my eyes and the faces of many people I've met pass by me: ten-year-old Libby at the musical *Riverdance,* joyously balancing on the edge of her seat, cheering for the scenes she liked; a woman telling me how she sang as she gave birth to her child; two young Jewish women taking the risk to invite me to their Seder meal; the compassionate nurse genuinely caring about his patients; the director of a large shelter showing great respect for each homeless person; a recently widowed Italian shoe-repair man on the plane chatting away his fear of flying; being respected as a minority while I sat among a large room full of black strangers waiting to board a plane at Abidjan on the Ivory Coast.

Immigrants especially remind me of the bigger world of our diversity. The supermarket where I shop in Des Moines has almost twenty different ethnic groups represented among the personnel. I like being there mixed in with them. I draw inspiration and hope from their courage in trying to adapt to a new country, to learn the language, and to be at home amid the strangeness of it all.

Some cultures have wonderful greeting customs that easily remind them of the sacredness of the other person and of their essential unity. An Irish priest told of a tribe in Nigeria who greet one another by first touching their hand over their own heart and then extending that hand outward to the other person as an extension of their heart's love and respect. I often use the "Namaste" greeting of India as I begin a retreat or a conference talk. Namaste means, "I greet the sacred in you. I look beyond the external judgments I might make about you. I see more deeply that you are a sacred being." When we sing this to one another a significant change happens among the group. We begin to look at one another with new eyes.

The cosmic dance has helped me to recognize this sacredness in the people of my world, to view them as part of an eternal movement of love. We are one vast web of intimate connection, all sailing on the same planet, in a universe threaded with the wonder of enriching diversity.

❧

Different from Me

thousands of them, different from me,
holding hands, kissing,
arms around each other,
stretching me beyond my own
safe world of heterosexuality,
a gathering of lesbians challenging me
to enter a world I never visit.

Being out of my comfort zone
takes me beyond my perception
of what is good, real, and true,
to the place where I can welcome
different ways of living and thinking,
even if I do not understand them.

I need to keep moving into
worlds unknown to me,
keep stretching, challenging
my judgmental mind, cleansing
my smudged view of reality.

I cannot understand what it is like
to be another race, color, nationality,
but I can turn my heart
toward awareness of our oneness,
and accept the beauty
of diversity.

A Snake or a Rope?

The Buddha explained that in the dark, you see a snake, you scream. But when you have a light, you see it is a rope. Sometimes we see a person as a snake, whereas she is only a rope. When I change my perception of the situation, my anger is transformed. —Sr. Chan Khong

I.

At 6:00 a.m. on Saturday morning the seventy-year-old across the street gets on his riding lawn mower and begins the noisy back and forth trips across the growing grass that he has carefully nurtured. My ears feel relieved when he gets to the far edge of the front lawn and heads toward the back of the yard for a minute. Then, around he comes again with another affront to my ears. The worst is the weed cutter that follows with its persistent buzz. This is followed by the leaf blower's whine as he pushes the cut grass off of the sidewalk. All this, while I am at meditation thinking, "that idiot can't wait 'til later to do this?" Only long after my non-loving response do I learn that his wife was dying in a hospice where he went early to be with her all day.

II.

I braved the ice, sleet, and snow to meet Sally at a café where we had met once before for lunch. I waited thirty minutes, silently blaming her for not showing up. She never came. I thought to myself, "Typical. She's so space-y. Always late. Often forgets." I ordered and ate my lunch and came home. As I left, I said to the waitress: "Well, she's notorious for being late." When I returned to my office I had a phone message waiting for me. It was Sally. She was still waiting at another café, the one where we had mutually agreed to meet and that I had forgotten to write on my calendar.

III.

The man who was our host was cold and inhospitable at the conference. I thought I could not stand another minute of his rudeness. I complained to a friend of his. I learned that our host had just been through a year of being falsely accused of sexual abuse, lost some trusted friends, nearly lost his job and his mind. He was still trying to recover his balance and had no idea how distant and aloof his manner was.

IV.

We were negotiating a contract for my future facilitation of an event. She sent me a message with hostile innuendoes. It seemed strange, given the circumstances and the facts. I wrote back and questioned why I felt attacked and misjudged. Then the truth came out. She was worried sick about the organization's finances and afraid to say so. On top of that her mother was very ill and she felt she should have flown home to be with her. She wasn't the harsh director I had imagined, just a woman with too much on her mind and heart.

Snakes and ropes. Sadly, I often mistake one for another.

Prisoners

they walk in with their tan uniforms,
while the five of us "visitors"
walk in with our identity badges.

I look around the group
and think to myself:
"If we left our badges and uniforms
outside the door
no one would ever know who's who."

Ethnic heritage, life situations,
personality patterns, clouded dreams,
choices and decisions made wrongly,
who can say just what it was
that brought these women here.

I feel compassion in a new way,
one among them, not apart,
at home with them,
and unafraid,
knowing them to be my sisters,
not just "prisoners of the state."

The Gift of People

People continually come into my life at just the right moment. Some come to teach, others to comfort, some to challenge, and some to affirm. Some people offer me help when I am struggling, some give direction when I am searching, and others bring me home to myself when I have gotten lost in the endless tasks of life.

Some of these people come in the shape of strangers, others as authors of books. Some are members of my family or religious community, while other people who show up to touch my life are faithful friends, understanding colleagues, and wise counselors.

People come in all sorts of packages, small and tall, heavy and thin, young and old. Some of them speak other languages, have colored hair, some have no hair at all. Some smile a lot and others are serious. Some are outrageously loud and others are quietly serene.

When I've doubted my writing abilities, an affirming letter from a reader sets me straight again. Finding myself running through an airport, a cleaning woman guides me to an elevator and helps me to a departure gate. When I've grieved the sudden death of a loved one, a composer's comforting song helps me to endure. Longing to be a part of a weekly ritual group, along comes a woman on retreat who has yearned for the very same thing and together we start a new adventure. When a tire blows out on my car on the highway, there's someone I trust who gives me a hand.

Children bring me back to the laughter in my life. Dying people help me put my life in perspective and reclaim my values. Workers on night shifts, those who stand long hours in factories, and those holding two or three jobs to make enough to live on, show me how easy I have it. Men and women who struggle with chronic illness or have tiptoed on the thin line of survival from a life-threatening disease show me what determination is. Explorers who brave the edges of unknown worlds rekindle the fire of my limp courage. Faith-filled people seed my anxiety with trust. People from other cultures and lands expand my horizons and remind me of the miracle of humanity's endless possibility.

When I reflect upon my death and departure from this beautiful planet, I sometimes say that it is Earth's beauty I will most regret leaving. However, just when I get to thinking in this way, I realize it is also the people of my life whom I will greatly miss. How much I have learned, how often I have been comforted, how many times I have experienced joy, and how much I have grown because of the presence of other people in my life.

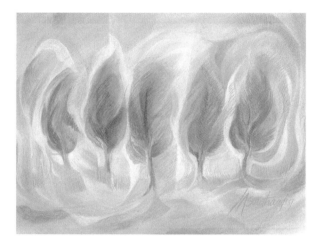

Autumn Lamp

late October, walking alone
in upstate New York,
my friend Leanna dying two days before,
much too young to make that long journey,
but who am I to say?

spacious tall maple tree, flawlessly shaped,
a sphere of gentle yellow pierced
by afternoon sun, each leaf a lantern glowing,
veneration the only response.

standing before such beauty comes
the deep breath of tender remembrance.

she and the tree, a lamp of autumn,
illuminating presence, beauty far and deep,
eyes shining love, strong embrace,
holding each one close to her cheek
(what strength she had, to the very end).

a soul aglow,
set ablaze by inner illumination,
readying, readying for the long journey.
the soul goes, the last leaf falls,
and I remember
the power of her shining.

Walking with the Aged

you thought you were
doing her a favor,
taking her, cane and all,
on the walk
through the deep woods,
helping her move along
November paths
carpeted with remnants
of summer's finery.

you thought nothing
of what she would bring to you
until she paused
at the creek's edge
and asked,
"Do you think our grandchildren
will get to see this beauty?
I love all this so much.
I take nothing for granted."

you eased up on your thoughts
about you being the one to do the giving,
but she wasn't finished.

down the slope, across the creek,
she cried, "Look, bittersweet,
there on that far branch!"
how many times had you walked
that timeless wooded path
and never saw? too fast to see.

it was then you knew
you were definitely not the one giving
and decided
it was time to receive.

Chapter 7

PAIN AND DESTRUCTION

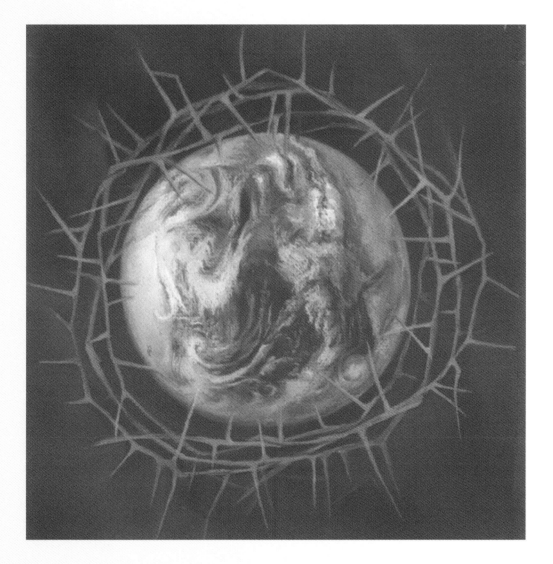

What Have You Done to Me?

...from day to night
you bring me to an end.
                    IS 38:13B

I am the spawning salmon
too weak to swim upstream

I am the sickened song bird
dying from pesticides

I am the unprotected top soil
ripped away by swirling rains

I am the great rivers and lakes
invaded by murky garbage

I am homeless creatures
searching for a lost habitat

I am the emptied rain forest
weeping from being raped

I am the gentle dolphin
tangled in gluttonous fishing nets

I am the graceful antelope
hit by the speeding vehicle

I am all species of plant and creature
threatened, poisoned, destroyed

I am Earth, your nurturing Mother,
wounded and in sore distress

Who will hear my cry?
Who will bear my sorrow?
Who will come to my aid?
Who will free me from my pain?

The difficulty is that…
we began to think of the universe
as a collection of objects
rather than as a communion of subjects.
Thomas Berry

As we get to know the sea, mountains, people, creatures, and other inhabitants of Earth, we learn their stories, see where they have been weakened by illness and accidents, discover the pains they have endured in the storms and struggles of life and unexpected events. We learn that death is inevitable, no matter how closely and carefully people and nature are guarded and tended. Natural disasters such as earthquakes, tornadoes, and hurricanes occur because of climatic and seasonal changes. Animals and plants feed on one another in order to live. Everything ages and weakens. Life and death follow one another in a natural cycle and from this cycle new life is eventually birthed.

However, a tremendous amount of pain and destruction is cruel and often preventable. Deaths, meaningless deaths, unwarranted deaths, careless deaths and deliberately callous deaths—they happen all the time. Humans do this to one another and they do this to their environment as well. Soil is washed away due to careless farming practices. Fish die because large factories pollute their waters with refuse. Birds and sea creatures struggle helplessly in huge spills of oil tankers. Limbs of orphaned children are blown to bits by land mines. Humans are lined up and murdered, their bodies thrown into mass graves. The priceless life of many is cut short, all because of attitudes and actions that hasten death and cause needless, excruciating suffering.

Humans have long thought of themselves as superior to the rest of creation and this thinking has promulgated a false sense of authority and dominance, creating the illusion that humans are "better than" and "apart from", rather than intimately connected with the rest of life. Rachel Carson, who first awakened society to the harm that humans were wreaking upon the land through pesticides, wrote: "The control of nature is a phrase conceived in arrogance born out of the Neanderthal age…when it was supposed that nature exists for the convenience of man."[1]

---

[1] *Silent Spring*, Rachel Carson. Houghton Mifflin Co., New York, 1962, p. 297.

Thomas Berry observed that many humans see the world as a collection of things rather than as sacred sources of existence, as individual objects rather than as a part of one great organism in which the experience of each affects the life of all.[2] Humans have become used to taking what they want from Earth without considering the consequences. Much of the unnecessary planetary pain today is caused by humans seeking their own convenience and comfort at the expense of Earth. "Forget the trees, air, water, soil, and creatures," human actions seem to say, "just let us have more shopping malls, larger houses, numerous electrical gadgets, wider highways, water fountains in desert cities . . . "

Something that has helped me in changing my own "dominance attitude" was learning how to "think like a mountain."[3] With this approach, I discovered a way to enter into the life and death of nature by trying to "get inside" what nature was experiencing. I did this by pausing and being present, thinking what it must be like to be a tree enduring many seasons and then quickly cut down, to be the sea with tons of garbage continually shoved into it, to be a mountain when the ancient stones and soil are roughly cut aside to form a road, to be an elk hunted and killed, to be a sea otter whose family faces extinction.

When I began to think in this way, I discovered a creation composed not of "things," or "objects," but of sacred companions with as much a right to live and exist as I have.

Because of my changed consciousness, I had a whole different awareness when I read about the grizzly bear's struggle for survival and learned that these great bears have seen their habitat shrink to less than one percent of their former range. I could imagine their loss and hunger as they searched to find a home and enough food for survival. I thought: "It's like if I had been living in a huge estate and now had to live in a closet."

Likewise, I understood the anguish in the voice of a farmer in Wales as she described her sorrow in having her whole herd of cows, three generations of Herefords, shot and killed at the time of the foot and mouth epidemic. With tears streaming down her cheeks she said she knew each of the cows by name and that even if she was blindfolded she would know them by touching their udders from her years of milking them. She knew they had to be killed because they were dying, the skin on their tongues and udders was falling off from the disease.

I understood her grief as well as the suffering of her cows because each part of Earth pains in its own way. All of life is sacred and

---

[2] *The Great Work: Our Way into the Future*, Thomas Berry. Bell Tower, New York: 1999.
[3] *Thinking Like a Mountain*, John Seed, Joanna Macy, Pat Fleming, Arne Naess. New Society Publ, PA, 1988.

deserves to be treated with dignity and respect. When creatures and plants generously give their lives so that others might live, those who receive life from them need to do so with awareness and gratitude, remembering the sacrifice that has been made for them.

The pain of Earth and the destructive tendencies of humans are many and will not be easily solved. There are no quick solutions to the problems that exist. For example, how can we make a choice between large river dams that supply vast amounts of electricity and needed irrigation, and the destruction of habitat for millions of fish and other creatures that these dams create? How can we protect the Arctic coastal plains of Alaska, still untamed and rich with herds of caribou, wolves, bears, birds and other wildlife, and also find a way to meet the need of fuel consumers by drilling intrusive oil wells in that area? Creative solutions to the many environmental dilemmas must be sought with unselfish compromise, with an attitude of what is best for ALL involved, always with an awareness of the oneness of life that we share.

We cannot go on as before, none of us. Each action we take has an influence on the rest of life on the planet. Nothing we do remains isolated. Each influences the other. It is a tremendous gift and also, an enormous challenge. As long as Earth remains an "it," a "thing," rather than a living, vibrant reservoir of life, humans will continue to use and abuse her. We need a loving relationship with this generous, vulnerable planet on which we live. Only then will we allow her songs of rich abundance to dance in the rhythms of our lives, only then will we respond with reverent care and live with daily gratitude.

Wild Ones

Wild ones still grow
in secret corners.
They dance with passion
where no one has come
with machines that hack,
cut, gather, and destroy.

Wild plum trees,
tall prairie grass,
stickery seeds,
red berry bushes,
and all sorts of
untamed vegetation.

Wild with rejoicing,
they sing in secrecy,
hide in unsought valleys,
dream in quiet oak groves,
whisper in forgotten fields.

They dwell,
these wild ones,
on the plains,
the mountains,
and some as near
as a few blocks
from the last concrete slabs
of the suburbs.

Who will protect
these wild ones
from those who slay
in the name of taming?
Who will keep them free
from those who destroy
for the sake of comfort?

The Eyes of Starving Children

late autumn parish dinner,
plates piled high with food,
I stood at my dutiful position
in the hot, sweltering kitchen
readying dishes for the washer,
the torrent of hot water
pushing slice after slice
of leftover roast beef
down the huge disposal.
Desserts hardly touched,
halves of fresh wheat bread,
little clumps of cabbage salad,
green beans, and mashed potatoes,
all of it swooshed down the drain
to be masticated and destroyed
in the strong jaws of metal.

Three long hours I stood there
emptying plate after plate of food
while the well-fed burped,
and the eyes of starving children,
with their bloated stomachs,
watched my every move.

Entering the Pain of Another

Compassion means to come close to the one who suffers . . .
A compassionate person says, "I am your brother;
I am your sister; I am human, fragile, and mortal, just like you . . ."
We can be with the other only when the other ceases to be other
and becomes like us.—Henri Nouwen

Native Americans have a saying that we must walk a mile in someone else's moccasins in order to know what that person is experiencing. When someone I know and care about is in pain I can readily walk in their moccasins and extend compassion to them but how much more challenging it is when the "suffering one" is part of a person or group whom I consider either an enemy or a separate entity. This was never so clear to me as when I entered a side chapel in the beautiful Imperial Cathedral in Aachen, Germany. A touching statue of Mary, the Mother of Sorrows, with seven swords piercing her heart, was the centerpiece of this chapel. I sat there for some time, aware of a presence that was unusual and filled with palpable, unspoken grief. I wondered why I felt it so strongly there.

It was not until later that I discovered the chapel was dedicated to the mothers of those who had lost their sons and daughters fighting as Nazis in WWII. I was stunned and felt great remorse. Why had I never considered these grieving women whose heartache was all as great as those who had lost sons and daughters fighting for the Allies? It was, of course, because I had never allowed myself to think of them as part of my cosmic life. I had never

allowed myself to enter into their pain. I had kept them at a great distance from myself.

A pastor once said that every CEO should have to work in a packing plant or at a common job for awhile, like every physician should have to be a patient. These comments came after an article about a news anchor who was described as being a smug, cold-hearted person until his four-year-old daughter developed leukemia. Suddenly he saw how precious life was and what people had to cope with when they were going through tough situations. Now, when he does interviews and stories, he approaches hurting people with much greater understanding and kindness. He said he now realizes the immense value of loved ones and what it is like to suffer the loss of them.

When we enter into the suffering of others we enter into the cosmic dance of their pain. It is a tender dance of tears inviting each of us to enter it with compassion for our brothers and sisters everywhere. When we draw near to those who suffer, we enter into this cosmic dance in a deep and powerful way. We embrace mystery and enter into a compassionate love that stretches far beyond our own heart, joining with the One Great Heart that beats endlessly in our vast universe.

Uprooted

long ragged lines
of lost people
wrap around
the wide boundaries of Earth,
like roots seeking soil
after a deluging erasure.

day after day they walk,
trudging onward, leaving behind
the little or the much
they once had.

a multitude of refugees
departing, fleeing
from whatever has loosened
their bond with the past.

poverty-worn workers trying to cross
unwelcome borders, seeking jobs,
homeless ones walking away from rubble and debris,
tattered by earthquakes, fires, floods,

the terrified running from rebels and dictators,
others fleeing the chaos of uncertainty
and wounds too old, too deep to heal.

the ugly whip of pain and destruction
forces the long lines forward,
rootless and unpretentious,
allowing them little time to glance backward
at what they leave behind.

they look ahead with anxious eyes,
eyes that only the emptied can understand,
wondering if they will find a place
where roots grow strong
and home is undisturbed.

Broken Boulders

Limestone chunks,
garnered from the Kansas soil,
stand in a tall circle of ceremony,
high on the meadow's crown.

Rain and wind weakened,
some have collapsed,
fallen from the silent circle,
a heap of brokenness
on a grassy hillside,
while others with huge cracks
soon approach the day of descent.

Some grow old and stay strong,
others grow old and fall apart,
the same substance, aging differently.

Like people. JoDee dead at 55.
Suz alive and going strong at 96.
Does it make any sense?
Logic is simply out of the question here.
Live each day well. Be prepared
for the final passage, never knowing

when the boulder will crack,
collapse to the ground,
and dissolve back into Earth.

Separation from Earth

Each one of us matters, has a role to play,
makes a difference...Together we must reestablish
our connections with the natural world and with
the Spiritual Power that is around us. — JANE GOODALL

The way of life in which people were easily in tune with nature is rapidly disappearing. People work in offices that have no natural air or outdoor light, study in classrooms without windows, drive in cars equipped with videos which occupy children and cause them to miss the natural scenes of life, travel to work on underground transit trains or on clogged, concrete freeways with views of billboard signs. Indoor exercise machines replace walking and jogging in the open air. People of all ages spend hours in front of computers and television sets, stepping outside only to get the mail or newspaper, hurriedly moving in and out of buildings when shopping or going to work, rarely noticing the environment around them. It frightens me because the more we lose touch with Earth, the less sense we have of our relationship with her and with her life-giving qualities.

We need to be with nature. When we are constantly indoors we forget and fail to notice the wonders that lie beyond those closed doors.

It is easy and natural to simply use and abuse Earth and her resources, to pollute, damage, and never enter into a relationship involving care and compassion for her treasures because we are rarely aware of those treasures.

If we ignore the beauty and abundance of Earth who will teach and inspire our children to learn from and appreciate Earth's goodness? How will anyone realize the immense dance that unites us with all of life? Who will draw comfort from the soft air of a springtime evening? Who will be encouraged by seeing crocuses rise up through the snow? Who will be inspired by the full moon rising over the city? Who will see the miracles of growth that happen every day in flowers that bud and bloom? Who will feel the delight of a fresh rain? Who will be enthralled by a rabbit chewing a blade of grass? Who will hear the communal honking of a flock of geese? Who will touch the downy softness of a new foal? Who will be tantalized by a juicy, red strawberry in the garden? Who will commune with the fireflies and laugh at the antics of squirrels?

Not those who are constantly cooped up indoors. Not those who keep their senses aloof from creation. Not those who forget the rhythm of the seasons and the secret wonders of nature. Not those who have lost touch with the power in a seed and the beauty of a sunset.

We need to be with Earth, listen to her humming in the music of her creatures, sway with her dancing in the wintry branches of snow-filled trees, embrace the ebb and flow of her seas, breathe in the fresh air of her mornings and the mellow scent of her flowers. We must reach out, gaze upon, touch, walk, sit, and enjoy the colors, shapes, and sounds of the natural world, lest in ignoring these beauties they are all too soon lost to us forever.

Life and Death

the nest sits empty
in the honeysuckle bush,
abandoned
by attentive parents.
long faithful days
of warming the egg
now lost to the fat cat
that preys in my back yard.

the egg hatched,
the parents eagerly fed,
carefully tended,
but the silent prowler
stalked the powerless
and devoured the newborn.

I still detest this reality,
the cycle of life and death
with its Kali[1] obliteration,
pouncing upon the unprotected,
harshly interrupting life,
annihilating the powerless,
devastating the seed of beauty.

But death continues to enter in
with the cinders of defeat,
and for a long while it seems
nothing will ever grow again.

---

[1] A Hindu goddess, part of a threefold process of creation, preservation, and destruction, usually acknowledged most for her ability to destroy. She is honored as an essential aspect of the transformation process.

Chapter 8

HOPE

Behold This Newborn Child

Each time a child is born,
particularly after a grandparent dies,
we sense that life goes on.
All is not lost.
There is a deep resilience,
stronger than the grasp of death.

The babe is lifted high
toward the welcoming stars,
a young life
with just a kernel of ripening,
a new resident
in the heart of existence.

All those gathered proclaim:

"Behold, behold, this newborn one!
Let us nurture and keep alive
the sacred mystery of hope
hallowed in this young one's heart.
We sow our dreams of a future
in this freshly birthed being.
We give our loving promise
to guide and guard this child.
Always we will remember
our oneness in the dancing cosmos."

The stars say not a word.
They bow in reverence
to this creature,
whose adult hands will hold
power enough
to blow up a planet,
or seed a waiting garden.

The stars smile,
for they too have hope,
and night
turns toward the dawn.

Faith in the future is not dead in our hearts.
Better still, it is this hope, deepened and purified,
which seems bound to save us.
Teilhard de Chardin

When difficulties and misfortune occur there is always the possibility of becoming bitter, hostile, and fearful. On the other hand, there are those who gradually move beyond the overwhelming loss and come to accept hope in their hearts, trusting they will get through the pain and find some kind of positive growth because of what they have experienced. It is true that some things can never be recovered. Loved ones die, accidents cause permanent impairment, species are terminated, natural resources are gone forever. Yet, I believe in hope. My own experience, along with many wounded people who have shared their stories of subsequent growth and healing with me, has convinced me of the necessity of having hope.

I also believe in the power of hope because I have seen Earth survive terrible blows and recover from significant distress. Amid the pain and struggle, the raw wounds of violence and the poisonous harm being done to our planet and to individuals, there are numerous reasons to continue to have hope in the future.

A huge amount of goodness rests in the hearts of humankind and much resilience shines through the innermost part of creation.

The yearning toward life is strong and deep in nature. The pattern in creation is one of transformation: out of death comes life. The seasons teach us this as do many other aspects of nature. A dry, brown seed is pressed into a dark space of soil and there it gestates into a new green shoot. An old saguaro cactus with many holes in the arms and trunk lives on and provides a habitat for a variety of creatures. Bushes of green beans given up for dead in the dry garden blossom again after an inch of rain. A three-legged doe, the fourth leg broken and held high, births two young fawns and nurtures them. A flooded cornfield yields a generous crop the following year. Fireweed grows on a mountainside after a devastating fire. Determined grass pushes its way up through the cracks of a concrete parking lot. A green shoot emerges out of a dead tree stump.

Humans also experience the power of transformation. A pregnant Mozambique woman is caught in a raging flood. She spends three days in a tree where she not only survives but also gives birth to a healthy child while in that tree. Others in harsh situations also make it through them. People with serious illness, thwarted dreams, lost jobs, violated bodies, trampled spirits, and grief so deep it penetrates to the core of the soul, gradually return to a sense of peace and acceptance. Those who lose homes in floods, fires, or earthquakes slowly put the pieces of their lives back together. It may take a long time but something deep inside tells them they must go on, that there is more of life yet to live. The voice of hope tells them they can move on into the future. It asks them to trust in the possibility of unfolding happiness even if they can never reclaim what has been lost.

We often do not know until years later how something seemingly hopeless might positively influence the future. Roger and Mary Williams, founders of Rhode Island, were buried side by side in a grave close to where an apple tree was planted. Many years later the local residents wanted to exhume the bodies and bury them with honor but when they excavated the graveside they discovered that the bodies had completely decayed, even the bones. The roots of the apple tree had fed on the phosphorus of the decaying bones and changed the human substance into food for the tree. Even in death, life goes on to nurture the future. Hope prevails.[1]

A new consciousness of how we need to treat Earth and humankind continues to grow and widen. There is a greater awareness of how Earth has been harmed and there is a stronger desire to help her heal from this harm. More individuals are recycling materials, adopting stretches of roads and highways to keep them litter-free, planting trees, using natural resources with greater care and conservation. People are coming closer to nature by gardening, hiking, and other outdoor activities. Legislators are passing environmental laws. Numerous national and international organizations are raising issues and writing charters about systemic changes and attitudes that are needed in order to protect and save our planet.

Farmers are using contour cultivation, hillside terracing, crop rotation, and minimum tillage while conservation corps are reconstructing prairies and wetlands to prevent flooding and protect topsoil. Cities are developing parks, financing recycling programs, and saving "green space" to guard the land from urban sprawl. Environmentally conscious industries are creating new products that use less of Earth's precious resources and others are taking greater care with the disposal of toxic refuse. Much, much more needs to be done to raise awareness, alter attitudes, and change behaviors on behalf

---

[1] *Dirt: The Ecstatic Skin of the Earth*, William Bryant Logan. Riverhead Books, NY, 1995, p. 57.

of our planetary home but positive beginnings are being nurtured.

There are many who work for the good of our world. This solidarity is an important part of hope, reminding us of our shared values and dreams. Russian cosmonaut Oleg Makarov reflected on how, from outer space, it was easy to see our external solidarity, to view Earth not as many separate, distant countries but as "one touchingly small sphere." From out there he saw our unity.[2]

Teilhard de Chardin named our internal unity when he wrote: "We are all of us together carried in the one world-womb."[3] This solidarity with all that exists is a great source of hope. In this amazing web of oneness there is the unique beauty, power, and resilient dynamism of an interwoven existence. Our oneness in the great dance of life is a tremendous strength. It urges us to live and act in ways that are beneficial for all. It tells us that a sustainable future is possible, one in which everything and everyone lives in harmony, assured of a safe environment in which to grow and mature. We cannot give up hope. We need to foster a deep assurance that the beauty, joy, and nourishment that Gaia, our beloved Earth, offers us will continue far into the future.

I once walked in ankle-deep water across the small, narrow source of the great Mississippi River in northern Minnesota. As I did so, I thought of the myriad streams and tributaries that join to make a wide, vigorous river. Like that river, everyone and everything is joined in the dancing water of the cosmos. Individually we are small rivulets but united we are a mighty river held in one great embrace by the Source of All Goodness. Together we are strong. Together we have hope. Together we will grow. Together we will co-create a world that dances in harmony and love.

❧

[2] *The Home Planet,* ed. Kevin W. Kelley. Addison-Wesley Publ. Co., NY, 1988.
[3] *Building the Earth,* Teilhard de Chardin. Dimension Books, Wilkes-Barre, PA 1965, p. 122.

How Did They Know?

How did they know
it was time to push up
through the long-wintered soil?

How did they know
it was the moment to resurrect
while thick layers of stubborn ice
still pressed the bleak ground flat?

But the tulips knew.
They came, rising strongly,
a day after the ice died.

There's a hope-filled place in me
that also knows when to rise.
It is urged by the strong sun
warming my wintered heart.
It is nudged by the Secret One,
calling, calling, calling,
"Arise, my love, and come."

Like the dormant tulips
my heart stirs,
and hope comes dancing forth.

Not unlike the Holy One
kissing the morning sun,
waving a final farewell
to a tomb emptied of its treasure.

Dancing Circles of Hope

everywhere women are dancing

long, black braids flying freely
to a rhythmic chant of happiness
on the hills of Korea

women stepping into a circle
of celebration as they lift their canoes
out of Wisconsin's boundary waters

beating flat drums
beside the glowing coals
of South Dakota ceremonies

leaping and swaying in darkness
on the bushland of the Kalahari

wailing stories of grief
in the circles of Bosnia and Rwanda

gathering by Celtic sites in the British Isles
humming songs stored
in ancestral hearts

moving in one sacred step
repeating zikrs of Sufis
in the candlelight of their homes

voices and feet carrying hope one to another
while the frayed edge of the cosmos sighs
comforted by their melodies
for they hold the ancient mysteries
forgotten and discarded

they dance the delight of cosmic beauty
they dance to keep the story alive
they dance for those unable to dance
in body or in spirit

moving in circles of love
too strong to ever die

A Thousand Roots [1]

the poet Rilke knew
where to find hope
and why

God is dark, he said,
and like a wondrous web,
a thousand roots
with their hungry mouths
silently sipping

someday I'd like to slip
my head beneath the cover
of earth,
not the six-foot-deep type,
only far enough to see

to let my eyes behold those
sipping, slurping roots,
the tiny feathered ones,
the thick grandfathers,
the long maiden tendrils,
and the bulbous pregnant ones

to listen as they imbibe
delicious moisture
held inside that darkened space

I'd like to take a ride
through the hopeful web,
follow the fresh drink
still moist on the root's mouth,
travel up the green stem,
and hear the sigh of joy
in the fluttering, receptive leaves

[1] See Rilke's *Book of Hours*, trans. Anita Barrows and Joanna Macy (Riverhead Books, 1996) for Rainer Maria Rilke's poem in which he uses this phrase.

The Resilient Spirit

We are afflicted in every way, but not crushed;
perplexed, but not driven to despair;
persecuted, but not forsaken;
struck down, but not destroyed . . .   2 Cor 4:8-9

The sharp delineation of seasonal changes in the Midwest helps me believe in the resiliency of the human spirit. When I walk through the woods amid the stark, barren branches in late autumn or drive along seemingly dead, brown fields stripped of grain, I know that a vibrant green springtime will follow. The barrenness of the land with its inherent promise of new life assures me that I, too, can endure through a silent, empty season, that I, too, have a suppleness to my spirit which will help me bounce back after being flattened by the unwanted and inevitable struggles of life.

Resiliency is rooted in the human heart. It is an essential catalyst for moving through painful and devastating experiences. Resiliency is about being down and out and springing back, being persistent in the face of defeat. It is solidarity with others that strengthens the soul. It is hope that holds on in spite of overwhelming loss. It is unrelenting faith in a loving divinity whose abiding presence provides strength through every season.

I thought a lot about resiliency a few years ago when I went to visit my aunt in California. That year the gardeners had pruned her lemon tree. On previous visits the tree was burgeoning with delicious fruit, branches so weighted they hung all the way to the ground. This particular year, however, the tree was pruned beyond recognition. Almost all the smaller branches were gone, leaving gray blunt stumps, nary a leaf anywhere. I could not imagine that tree ever producing lovely lemons again, but to my great surprise and joy, the lemon tree was green and full of fruit two years later when I returned.

How much we are like that harshly pruned lemon tree when, at the time of a devastating situation, we feel demolished with unspeakable pain. We can't imagine ever feeling good again. So much seems at an end—our joy, our contentment, our peace of mind. We forget in those horrible times, or perhaps have never understood until then, that we are also capable of immense resilience. We can only think of how much distress and hurt we are experiencing.

It is then that the courageous ability to "bounce back" rises up in us, urging us to stand strong. Something abiding and enduring in us stirs and calls: "You can make it through this even though you feel overcome and defeated." Long ago this resiliency was seeded in our soul. It will enable us to bounce back from what threatens to destroy us. It will help us rise up from whatever knocks us down.

Good Memories

Good memories carry my heart
through the bad times.

I close my eyes.
I am there again
in the sheltered cove,
wrapped in tender mist,
held by an ancient rhythm,
embraced by a dancing sea.

Something greater than pain
unites the sea and my soul,
the memory lingers in me
like a well-fed pelican.

The dancing ocean
carries me along
through soiled dreams
and old mistakes.

The comforting sound
of endless waves ebbs
and flows in my strained soul.

I am cradled in the water's dance
of strength, restored
by the sea's undying energy.

Good memories,
I cherish them,
returning often
to their hopeful home.

Calling in the Ancestors

come, ancient ones,
original guardians of this place,
come with the heart you wore
as you stood on this hallowed land,
you who easily tendered Earth,
holding her treasures with uncalloused care

come, great ancestors of First Nations,
come, wise ones of American Indians,
come, first walkers of songlines
in the Outback,
come, Maori of the long boats,
come, shamans and healers, tribes
of many languages and color,
come, teach us who have forgotten
the Mother who feeds us

come, tell us the ancient truths
you knew so well,
breathe whispers of wisdom
in hearts whose memories have lost
the beauty of simple things
and the wonder of unharmed landscapes

come, dream dreams of hope in us,
stir in us songs of the seas and rivers,
dance stories of reverence in our blood,
raise up a profound kinship in our souls,
guide us into strong circles of respect
for everything inhabiting our world

come, original guardians,
breathe fire into our tame bones
'til we, too, stand strong,
fierce in our determination
to dwell on our beloved planet
with gratitude as deep as yours

The Summer of the Butterflies

*I*t was in early May that the phone call came, unexpected and without warning. A good friend had been to see her physician and she called to tell me she had just been diagnosed with a possible brain tumor. A week later she learned the tumor was the type that grows quickly and leaves little room for hope of recovery.

That day of the terrible news I went out to sit on the deck in the midst of fresh spring air and greening trees, to try to absorb the harsh prognosis. As I was sitting there with a heavy heart, a monarch butterfly came with all its orange glory and perched on my hand. The butterfly just sat there. Silent and still. It was then I felt the heartbeat, a tiny pulse in the body of that beautiful creature. There we were, the two of us breathing, hearts beating, united. Something peaceful stirred in me and I knew that no matter what happened to Sandra, she would be all right.

All summer butterflies of dazzling colors and types kept me company. They sat in my hair and fluttered around me as I walked on city streets. Each time I sensed they were telling me about Sandra: "Do not worry. There is life after this one. She is journeying to another realm on the path of transformation. Do not be dismayed."

Two months after Sandra's diagnosis one of my brothers-in-law died of a heart attack. Another surprise. He was young and healthy, or so we supposed. The day after the funeral I traveled home and went to a friend's garden to pick some vegetables. As I leaned over and reached for a tomato, something caught my eye. I turned and gasped in amazement at what I saw. A huge, metallic blue, swallowtail butterfly was sitting on a large, orange zinnia. With the wings spread open the swallowtail was as large as the palm of my hand. I stood and gazed in absolute awe.

The butterfly sipped contentedly from the flower. Finally, I reached out and slowly touched the velvet of one blue wing. It seemed not to mind. Then the blue butterfly easily lifted and landed on a brilliant yellow zinnia where it once again busied itself with drinking nectar. I thought of my six foot seven inch brother-in-law who had recently died. I remembered my friend whose body was growing weaker. And I thought of the beautiful butterfly before me who had known the dark waiting womb of the chrysalis where a complete transformation had taken place. When I left the garden, I felt my understanding and acceptance of death, and the mystery of what follows it, strengthened in a deeply hopeful way.

A week or so later the daily newspaper carried an article about the astounding number of butterflies in the region that summer. No one was sure why they had come, not even the local entomologists. I did not know what had produced such a great number either, but for me, the timing could not have been better.

One Strong Star

I stand gazing at the cold winter sky,
thirty minutes after midnight
on the first day of the new year.
What I see catches my heart
and draws me into profound hope.

There in the black winter sky
one strong star sings a silent melody,
illuminating the heavily clouded heights
with a powerful, assuring presence.
I hear it calling to every human soul
whose life yearns for something more.

One strong star sends a brave song
to those who doubt their own courage.
It shines for the soreness of the planet
and for all who die daily
in their coffins of discouragement.

I stand gazing at that single star
resonating with the shining message:
none of us need doubt our ability to survive.

Hope comes in little ways,
it only takes one shining star,
one faithful friend,
one wisp of inspiration,
one touch of creation's beauty,
one deep sip of love,
to keep the illumination alive in us.

In the snow-laden clouds of the first day
of the new year
I bow to the heavens and turn homeward,
grateful for the quiet in my heart,
and for the singing of a lone star
sending strength
to every corner of the cosmos.

Afterword

by Mary Southard, CSJ

Where would we be without Earth wherein we "live and move and have our being," and dance and dream and love and grow? This holy place of divine indwelling feeds, shelters, and clothes us, and holds us safe in a loving embrace. Earth has brought forth the most wondrous array of living beings, especially these past 65 million years—flowers and trees, birds and insects, land and water mammals of every size and shape and color. This most glorious era of evolution awakens and nourishes the human spirit.

"Human intelligence requires a magnificent world, a beautiful world, a world of resonance and meaning," writes Thomas Berry. "For humans to bear the burden of intelligence and responsibility, we need a beautiful world to inspire and heal us." How true this has been for me. Ever since I was a child Earth has restored me to a sense of harmony and well being. Feeling the first warm breezes of spring blowing through my hair, watching snowflakes drift beneath a street light, walking through a field, sitting on our front porch of an evening would draw me into a Presence, a gentle peace.

Once, years later, during a frightening period of personal crisis I discovered that painting and praying with images of the living things of creation, their seeds and cycles, light and dark, winds and seasons, brought new meaning and the beginning of healing. Then I noticed that these were images of hope not only for me, but also for others. Art was becoming a way for me to participate in the processes of transformation at the heart of all life. I began to feel connected to the soul of the world.

Then the universe came roaring, dancing into my awareness! There was the agony of awakening to the scope of our ecological crisis, and at the same time the ecstasy of learning the scientific "New Story" of creation being discovered in all the sciences. I was stunned with the sacred beauty of this emerging revelation! I met Thomas Berry and Brian Swimme, first through their writings, then as friends and mentors on our human journey into a new worldview—so whole and spacious and beautiful, so full of creativity and compassion.

There was a farm in the beautiful hills of Wisconsin where I was blessed to be able to live alone for a year—to "learn from Earth." First thing in the morning I rose from my bed and went outdoors to stand "in earth," on the land, in order to remember who I am, to experience my intimate connection with all my relations, to ask to be open to and strengthened by divine energy flowing all around and within me. And I painted, and studied, and felt myself drawn into the New Story—the origin and nature of the Universe, more vast and ancient, more intimate and precise than anyone could have ever imagined! I contemplated the image of Earth from space glowing in velvet blackness, exquisitely beautiful, abundant, and fragile. How could I not have known that this is not a place of exile, but the garden, our home! I painted what it feels like to belong, to be a child of the universe, born of stardust, spiritually and physically kin with every other being that is. Each day the neighbor's dog would come and we would take long walks together, clearly fond of each other. Once again, in the way of a child, I was discovering life anew, falling in love again with Earth, with God!

But then would come the sadness, the anguish of knowing what we humans are doing to Earth and one another. I grieved the dangerous unraveling of life going on all around us—not yet recognized by a greedy consumer culture, politics, or media. I grieved human violence and planetary suffering, and I grieved for the children who will inherit such a diminished planet. The magnitude of what we are bringing about all but overwhelmed me at times, but painting and sculpting became a way to pray through the tears, to live my way into new ways of seeing and being. The call to make art became a way to wake up and stay awake, a way to dance the agony and the ecstasy of our moment in planetary evolution, a way to participate deeply in life and celebrate all its beauty and Mystery.

As I am drawn more completely into the dance, I delight in the great variety of dancing partners I meet there! Many moons ago Joyce Rupp and Mike Leach invited me to join them in the adventure of this book. Surprise and timidity soon gave way to the joy of dancing with these two who move with such grace and creativity through the process!

In her poetry, prayer, and praise, Joyce so beautifully invites us to experience God as Dancer, moving within all beings, dancing forth the creation, evolution—where everyone and everything is dancing with everyone and everything else. All are held gently in the arms of compassionate belonging, yet each is set free to explore and expand and bring forth new expressions of itself. The universe is a

dance, alive with holy energy that brings forth and engages all things in rhythmic relationship —stars and galaxies, suns and planets, birds and butterflies, winds, waters, and soil, toads, and humans—all in one grand harmonious dance! Earth is a Divine work of art in process, a poem unfolding, a song ever being sung, always bringing forth greater and greater expressions of beauty and love.

This I believe! Each of us is a dancer in this cosmic dance. Each being, each human alive today is here to participate in the creative adventure that is the universe. There can be no spectators. Some deep longing—each one's unique gift, a passion for belonging, our dream for a world of love and unity—is urging us to get up and dance!

Books by Joyce Rupp

Fresh Bread
Praying Our Goodbyes
The Star in My Heart
May I Have This Dance?
Little Pieces of Light
Dear Heart, Come Home
The Cup of Our Life
Your Sorrow Is My Sorrow
May I Walk You Home? (co-authored with Joyce Hutchison)
Prayers to Sophia
Out of the Ordinary
Inviting God In